Mark Batterson

AUTHOR OF *In a Pit with a Lion on a Snowy Day*

Wild Goose Chase

Reclaim the Adventure of Pursuing God

MULTNOMAH
BOOKS

WILD GOOSE CHASE
PUBLISHED BY MULTNOMAH BOOKS
12265 Oracle Boulevard, Suite 200
Colorado Springs, Colorado 80921

All Scripture quotations, unless otherwise indicated, are taken from the Holy Bible, New International Version®. NIV®. Copyright © 1973, 1978, 1984 by International Bible Society. Used by permission of Zondervan Publishing House. All rights reserved. Scripture quotations marked (ESV) are taken from The Holy Bible, English Standard Version, copyright © 2001 by Crossway Bibles, a division of Good News Publishers. Used by permission. All rights reserved. Scripture quotations marked (KJV) are from the King James Version. Scripture quotations marked (MSG) are taken from The Message by Eugene H. Peterson. Copyright © 1993, 1994, 1995, 1996, 2000, 2001, 2002. Used by permission of NavPress Publishing Group. All rights reserved. Scripture quotations marked (NLT) are taken from the Holy Bible, New Living Translation, copyright © 1996, 2004. Used by permission of Tyndale House Publishers Inc., Wheaton, Illinois 60189. All rights reserved.

Italics in Scripture quotations indicate the author's added emphasis.

Details in some anecdotes and stories have been changed to protect the identities of the persons involved.

ISBN 978-1-59052-719-1

Published in the United States by WaterBrook Multnomah, an imprint of The Crown Publishing Group, a division of Random House Inc., New York.

MULTNOMAH and its mountain colophon are registered trademarks of Random House Inc.

Library of Congress Cataloging-in-Publication Data
Batterson, Mark.
    Wild goose chase: reclaim the adventure of pursuing God/Mark Batterson.
        p. cm.
    ISBN 978-1-59052-719-1
    1. Christian life. I. Title.
    BV4501.3.B388 2008
    248.4—dc22

                                                            2008014984

Printed in the United States of America
2010

10 9 8 7

SPECIAL SALES
Most WaterBrook Multnomah books are available in special quantity discounts when purchased in bulk by corporations, organizations, and special interest groups. Custom imprinting or excerpting can also be done to fit special needs. For information, please e-mail SpecialMarkets@WaterBrookMultnomah.com or call 1-800-603-7051.

Praise for
Mark Batterson

"Mark Batterson's *Wild Goose Chase* detonates anemic Christianity masquerading as the 'real thing' and winsomely propels us to what can be and should be if we allow God's Spirit to be all He can be in our lives. Let it stretch you to greater things!"

—LOUIE GIGLIO, Passion Conferences, speaker and
author of *How Great Is Our God, Indescribable*,
and *I Am Not but I Know I AM*

"*Wild Goose Chase* puts the advent back in adventure, and frees us all to find out how risk can be another word for faith."

—LEONARD SWEET, Drew University, George Fox
University, sermons.com

"Mark Batterson is down-to-earth and humble—yet constantly pushes me to grow. I follow him as a leader, admire him as an innovator, and love him as a friend. Mark has become one of the most important voices for a new generation. Anything he touches changes lives."

—CRAIG GROESCHEL, pastor of Lifechurch.tv,
author of *Going All the Way*

"As a leader and teacher, Mark Batterson brings imagination, energy, and insight. Mark's genuine warmth and sincerity spill over into his communication, combining an intense love for his community with a passionate desire to see them living the life God dreams for them.

I appreciate his willingness to take bold risks and go to extraordinary lengths to reach our culture with a message that is truly relevant."

—ED YOUNG, senior pastor of Fellowship Church

"A thoughtful and energetic leader, Mark Batterson presses us to consider how we live out our faith in the world around us. When Mark has something to say, I am quick to listen."

—FRANK WRIGHT, PhD, president and CEO
of National Religious Broadcasters

"Mark's passion for God and our generation is contagious. His writing is honest and insightful. Go ahead—chase the lion and the wild goose—and you'll never be the same."

—MARGARET FEINBERG, author of *The Organic God*
and *The Sacred Echo*

"Mark Batterson is one of the church's most forward thinkers. In this book, he compels us to look both behind and ahead to discover answers to the 'whys' in our lives. *In a Pit with a Lion on a Snowy Day* helps us make sense of this beautiful mess we call life."

—LINDY LOWRY, editor of *Outreach* magazine

To my friend, mentor, and fellow Wild Goose chaser,
Dick Foth

Contents

CHAPTER I

Yawning Angels

Living a Life of Spiritual Adventure

Life is either a daring adventure, or nothing.
—Helen Keller

The Celtic Christians had a name for the Holy Spirit that has always intrigued me. They called Him *An Geadh-Glas,* or "the Wild Goose." I love the imagery and implications. The name hints at the mysterious nature of the Holy Spirit. Much like a wild goose, the Spirit of God cannot be tracked or tamed. An element of danger and an air of unpredictability surround Him. And while the name may sound a little sacrilegious at first earshot, I cannot think of a better description of what it's like to pursue the Spirit's leading through life than *Wild Goose chase.* I think the Celtic Christians were on to something that institutionalized Christianity has missed out on. And I wonder if we have clipped the wings of the Wild Goose and settled for something less—much less—than what God originally intended for us.

I understand that "wild goose chase" typically refers to a purposeless endeavor without a defined destination. But chasing the Wild Goose is different. The promptings of the Holy Spirit can sometimes *seem* pretty pointless, but rest assured, God is working His plan. And if you chase the Wild Goose, He will take you places you never could have imagined going by paths you never knew existed.

I don't know a single Christ follower who hasn't gotten stressed out over trying to figure out the will of God. We want to solve the mystery of the will of God the way we solve a Sudoku or crossword puzzle. But in my experience, intellectual analysis usually results in spiritual paralysis.

We try to make God fit within the confines of our cerebral cortex. We try to reduce the will of God to the logical limits of our left brain. But the will of God is neither logical nor linear. It is downright confusing and complicated.

A part of us feels as if something is spiritually wrong with us when we experience *circumstantial uncertainty*. But that is precisely what Jesus promised us when we are born of the Spirit and start following Him.[1] *Most of us will have no idea where we are going most of the time.* And I know that is unsettling. But circumstantial uncertainty also goes by another name: adventure.

I think it is only fair that I give a Wild Goose warning at the outset of this book: nothing is more unnerving or disorienting than passionately pursuing God. And the sooner we come to terms with that spiritual reality, the more we will enjoy the journey. I cannot, in good conscience, promise safety or certainty. But I *can* promise that chasing the Wild Goose will be anything but boring!

ISLANDS OF EDEN

Not long ago I visited what must be the closest thing to the Garden of Eden left on earth. It almost felt wrong arriving in the Galápagos Islands via airplane. Washing ashore on a bamboo raft would have seemed more apropos.

We spent most of our time island hopping in a boat that didn't seem large enough for the twelve people on board or the twelve-foot ocean waves we encountered. And sure enough, we discovered that the boat had capsized not long before our visit. That tidbit of information would have been nice to know before we climbed aboard— but it definitely added an element of adventure.

The entire week was full of new experiences. I went snorkeling for the first time and saw some of God's amazing underwater creations. Where did He come up with those color schemes? In an unscripted and unforgettable moment, my son Parker and I went swimming with some playful sea lions. And I accomplished one of my life goals by jumping off a forty-foot cliff into a narrow river gorge at Las Grietas. What an adrenaline rush!

The trip consisted of one adventure after another. So the saying in Spanish that we saw on a Sprite can that week seemed fitting, and we adopted it as our mantra: *Otro día, otra aventura.* Translation: "Another day, another adventure."

I love those four words inspired by Sprite. They capture the essence of what we experienced day in and day out in the Galápagos.

I think those words resonate with one of the deepest longings in the human heart—the longing for adventure. And I'm not sure I could come up with a better description of what it's like to pursue God.

Take the Holy Spirit out of the equation of my life, and it would spell b-o-r-i-n-g. Add Him into the equation of your life, and anything can happen. You never know who you'll meet, where you'll go, or what you'll do. All bets are off.

If you would describe your relationship with God as anything less than adventurous, then maybe you think you're following the Spirit but have actually settled for something less—something I call *inverted Christianity*. Instead of following the Spirit, we invite the Spirit to follow us. Instead of serving God's purposes, we want Him to serve our purposes. And while this may seem like a subtle distinction, it makes an ocean of difference. The result of this inverted relationship with God is not just a self-absorbed spirituality that leaves us feeling empty, it's also the difference between spiritual boredom and spiritual adventure.

CAGED CHRISTIANS

Situated five hundred miles off the coast of Ecuador, the Galápagos chain is one of the most primitive places on the planet. While many of the islands in the forty-nine-island archipelago are inhabited, most of them are absolutely undomesticated. When I was there, I felt as if I were as far from civilization as I could get. It was Edenic.

Somehow I felt a new affinity with Adam in the Galápagos environment. It helped me imagine what life must have been like before the Fall. Scripture tells us that one of the first jobs God gave Adam was naming the animals.[2] And we read right past it. But it must have taken years of research and exploration to complete the project. I don't think God paraded the animals past Adam in a single-file line; I'm guessing God let Adam discover them in their natural habitats. Imagine how thrilling it must have been for Adam to catch his first glimpse of wildebeests stampeding, mountain goats climbing, or rhinos charging.

That's how I felt when I was in the Galápagos. And it was there that I discovered the difference between seeing a caged animal at a local zoo and getting within arm's length of a mammoth marine iguana or walking a beach with hundreds of barking sea lions or floating above manta rays as they glide along the ocean floor. It's one thing to see a caged bird. It's an altogether different experience to see a pelican that looks like a prehistoric pterodactyl circling fifty feet above your boat, dive-bombing full speed into the ocean, and coming up with breakfast in its oversize beak.

Few things compare to the thrill of seeing a wild animal in its natural habitat. There is something so inspiring about a wild animal doing what it was created to do. Uncivilized. Untamed. Uncaged.

So a few weeks after returning from the Galápagos, our family spent an afternoon at the National Zoo near our home in Washington DC. It's a fantastic zoo. But it just wasn't the same after the Galápagos. I'm ruined for zoos. It's not the same seeing a caged animal. It's too safe. It's too tame. It's too predictable.

At one point we were walking through the ape house, and I had this thought as I looked through the protective Plexiglas window at a four-hundred-pound caged gorilla: *I wonder if churches do to people what zoos do to animals.*

I love the church. I bleed the church. And I'm not saying that the way the church cages people is intentional. In fact, it may be well intentioned. But too often we take people out of their natural habitat and try to tame them in the name of Christ. We try to remove the risk. We try to remove the danger. We try to remove the struggle. And what we end up with is a caged Christian.

Deep down inside, all of us long for more. Sure, the tamed part of us grows accustomed to the safety of the cage. But the untamed part longs for some danger, some challenge, some adventure. And at some point in our spiritual journey, the safety and predictability of the cage no longer satisfies. We have a primal longing to be uncaged. And the cage opens when we recognize that Jesus didn't die on the cross to keep us safe. Jesus died to make us dangerous.

Praying for protection is fine. I pray for a hedge of protection around my three children all the time. You probably pray that kind of prayer too. But when was the last time you asked God to make you dangerous?

I would like to think that when I pronounce the benediction at the end of our church services, I am sending dangerous people back into their natural habitat to wreak havoc on the Enemy.

LIVING DANGEROUSLY

Every once in a while, I have random thoughts that seem to come out of nowhere. Here's a thought that fired across my synapses not long ago: *Do angels yawn?*

I know it seems like an inane theological question, but I seriously wonder if angels have the capacity to get bored. More important, I wonder if some of us are living such safe lives that not only are *we* bored, but so are our guardian angels. If they could, would our guardian angels coax us out of our cage and beg us to give them something dangerous to do?

In the pages that follow you'll meet some dangerous people. Mind you, they're ordinary people. They have doubts and fears and problems just like you and me. But their courage to come out of the cage and live dangerously for the cause of Christ will inspire and challenge you to follow them as they follow the Spirit's leading.

I think of Ana Luisa, who used her award miles to fly to India and sacrificially serve some of the poorest of the poor at a medical clinic. I think of Mike, who started a dangerous ministry in a dangerous place—a porn show in Las Vegas. I think of Adam, whose sensitivity to the Wild Goose resulted in a life-changing encounter on a mission trip half a world away. And I think of Becky, who made a conscious decision to endanger her own life by becoming part of the crusade against human trafficking.

Since when did it become safe to follow Christ? Maybe it's time to come out of the cage and live dangerously for the cause of Christ.

SENSE OF ADVENTURE

The Danish philosopher and theologian Søren Kierkegaard believed that boredom is the root of all evil. I second the notion. Boredom isn't just boring; boredom is wrong. You cannot simultaneously live by faith and be bored. Faith and boredom are antithetical.

Against that backdrop, consider the gospel story of the rich young ruler. On paper the rich young ruler had it all: youth, wealth, and power. But something was still missing. The rich young ruler was bored with his faith. And I think it is evidenced by the question he asked Jesus: "What do I still lack?"[3]

I'll tell you exactly what he was lacking: spiritual adventure. His life was too easy, too predictable, and too comfortable. He kept all the commandments, but those commandments felt like a religious cage. I think there was a deep-seated longing within him for something more than simply not doing anything wrong.

Listen, not breaking the prohibitive commandments is right and good. But simply not breaking the prohibitive commandments isn't spiritually satisfying. It leaves us feeling caged. And I honestly think that is where many of us find ourselves.

Over the past decade, I have had the privilege of serving as lead pastor of National Community Church in Washington DC. As with every church, our demography and geography are unique. Seventy percent of NCCers are single twentysomethings navigating the quarterlife crisis. And most of them live or work on Capitol Hill. So the observation I'm about to share is undoubtedly shaped by the life stage of our congregation and the psyche of our city. But I also think human nature is human nature. And here is what I've observed: *many, if not most, Christians are bored with their faith*.

We know our sins are forgiven and forgotten. We know we will spend eternity with God when we cross the boundary of the space-time continuum. And we are trying our best to live our lives within the guardrails of God's good, pleasing, and perfect will. But still we have a gnawing feeling that something is missing.

I think the rich young ruler is representative of a generation that longs to come out of the cage and live dangerously for the cause of

Christ. But too many among us end up settling for spiritual medi-ocrity instead of striving for spiritual maturity. Jesus speaks to that deep-seated longing for adventure by challenging us to come out of the cage. But coming out of the cage means giving up the very thing in which we find our security and identity outside of Christ.

In the case of the rich young ruler, his cage was financial secu-rity. Jesus said to him, "If you want to be perfect, go, sell your pos-sessions and give to the poor, and you will have treasure in heaven. Then come, follow me."[4]

A part of us feels bad for the rich young ruler, right? How could Jesus demand so much? He asked him to give up everything he had! But we fail to appreciate the offer Jesus put on the table.

I live in the internship capital of the world. Every summer tens of thousands of young adults make the pilgrimage to DC to try and land the right internship with the right person because they know it can open the right door. It's amazing how many members of Con-gress were once congressional pages and how many Supreme Court justices were once Supreme Court clerks.

I don't care how much this rich young ruler had to give up—Jesus offered him so much more. This was the opportunity of a life-time: an internship with none other than the Son of God. Come on, that's got to look good on your résumé! You can't put a price tag on that kind of experience. But the rich young ruler turned it down. He opted for the cage. And he made the mistake so many of us make: he chose an accessorized life over a life of adventure, over a life of chasing the Wild Goose.

Now juxtapose the rich young ruler with the twelve undomesti-cated disciples who accepted the unpaid internship. They heard the parables with their own two ears. They drank the water Jesus turned into wine. They filleted the miraculous catch of fish. And they were there when Jesus turned the temple upside down, walked on water, and ascended into heaven.

In a day when the average person never traveled outside a thirty-five-mile radius of his home, Jesus sent His disciples to the four corners of the ancient world. These ordinary fishermen, who otherwise would have lived and died within sight of the Sea of Galilee, were sent to the ends of the earth as they knew it. What a Wild Goose chase! According to the third-century historian Eusebius, Peter sailed to Italy, John ended up in Asia, James the son of Zebedee traveled as far as Spain, and even doubting Thomas chased the Wild Goose all the way to India.

Just like the rich young ruler, we have a choice to make. The same offer is extended. We can stay in our cage, end up with everything, and realize it amounts to nothing. Or we can come out of our cage and chase the Wild Goose.

SIX CAGES

In the prequel to this book, *In a Pit with a Lion on a Snowy Day,* I retell the story of an ancient warrior named Benaiah to show how God wants us to chase the five-hundred-pound opportunities that come across our path. And I cite the aphorism "no guts, no glory." When we lack the guts to step out in faith, we rob God of the glory that rightfully belongs to Him.[5] In *Wild Goose Chase*, I want to take it a step further and show you how all of life becomes a grand adventure when we chase the trackless, matchless Goose of heaven. We'll retrace the steps of six Wild Goose chasers who come right out of the pages of Scripture. And my hope is that their footprints will guide us as we chase the Wild Goose. But before the chase begins, I do want to offer one simple reminder. This book is about more than you and me experiencing spiritual adventure. In fact, this book is not about you at all. It's a book about the Author and Perfecter of our faith,[6] who wants to write His-story through your life. And if you read through Scripture, you'll discover that His favorite genre is action-adventure.

Sure, you can choose the safety and predictability of the cage, forfeiting the adventure God has destined for you. But you won't be the only one missing out or losing out. When you lack the courage to chase the Wild Goose, the opportunity costs are staggering. Who might not hear about the love of God if you don't seize the opportunity to tell them? Who might be stuck in poverty, stuck in ignorance, stuck in pain if you're not there to help free them? Where might the advance of God's kingdom in the world stall out because you weren't there on the front lines?

Jesus' disciples didn't just live an exciting life post-Pentecost; they turned the world upside down.[7] And that's what you can be a part of too. *Wild Goose Chase* is an invitation to be part of something that is bigger than you and more important than you.

Are you in?

In the pages that follow I will identify six cages that keep us from roaming free with the Wild Goose and living the spiritual adventure God destined us to. I'm not sure which cages you may find yourself in. But the good news is this: you are only one Wild Goose chase away from the spiritual adventure God has destined for you.

The first cage is the *cage of responsibility.* Over the course of our lifetime, God-ordained passions tend to get buried beneath day-to-day responsibilities. Less important responsibilities displace more important ones. And our responsibilities become spiritual excuses that keep us from the adventure God has destined for us. Without even knowing it, we begin to practice what I call *irresponsible responsibility.* The Wild Goose chase begins when we come to terms with our greatest responsibility: pursuing the passions God has put in our heart.

The second cage, the *cage of routine,* is almost as subtle as the first. At some point in our spiritual journey, most of us trade adventure for routine. There is nothing wrong with a good routine. In fact, the key to spiritual growth is developing healthy and holy routines known as spiritual disciplines. But once a routine becomes routine, we need to disrupt the routine. Otherwise, sacred routines become empty rituals that keep us caged.

The third cage is the *cage of assumptions.* Our assumptions keep many of us from chasing the Wild Goose. *I'm too old. I'm too young. I'm underqualified. I'm overqualified. It's too late. It's too soon.* And the list goes on. As we age, many of us stop believing and start assuming. We stop living out of right-brain imagination and start living out of left-brain memory. And we put eight-foot ceilings on what God can do.

The fourth cage is the *cage of guilt.* The Enemy's tactics haven't changed since the Garden of Eden. He tries to neutralize us spiritually by getting us to focus on what we've done wrong in the past. Satan uses guilt to turn us into reactionaries. Jesus came to recondition our spiritual reflexes with His grace and turn us into revolutionaries for His cause. As long as you are focused on what you've done wrong in the past, you won't have energy left to dream kingdom dreams.

The fifth cage is the *cage of failure*. And, ironically, this is where many Wild Goose chases begin. Why? Because sometimes our plans have to fail in order for God's plans to succeed. Divine detours and divine delays are the ways God gets us where He wants us to go.

And the sixth and final cage is the *cage of fear*. We need to quit living as if the purpose of life is to arrive safely at death. Instead, we need to start playing offense with our lives. The world needs more daring people with daring plans. Why not you?

I want you to know that before you decided to read this book I started praying for you. I prayed that *Wild Goose Chase* would get into the right hands at the right time. So I hope this book is more than a casual read for you. It's a divine appointment waiting to happen. And I believe one chapter, one paragraph, or one sentence can change the trajectory of your life.

Let the chase begin.

Your Chase

- ⊛ What's your reaction to the ancient Celtic description of God as the "Wild Goose"—untamed, unpredictable, flying free?
- ⊛ How have you been living "inverted Christianity," trying to get God to serve your purposes instead of you serving His purposes?

✸ Right now, where are you on this spectrum?

| Playing | | Living dangerously |
| it safe | | for God |

✸ How does the call to spiritual adventure strike you?
What is it inside you that resonates with that call?

✸ Of the six cages described at the end of the chapter,
which do you think might apply to you the most
and why?

CHAPTER 2

Goose Bumps

Coming Out of the Cage of Responsibility

The soul lives by that which it loves.

—St. John of the Cross

A few years ago I figured out how I want to die. I know that sounds morbid and demands some explanation, so let me tell you how I came to my conclusion. I was reading about a man named Wilson Bentley.[8] I had never heard of him before. We have virtually nothing in common. And he died long before I was born. But when I discovered how he died, I determined that I want to die the same way Wilson Bentley died.

Wilson grew up on a farm in Jericho, Vermont, and as a young boy he developed a fascination with snowflakes. *Obsession* might be a better word for it. Most people go indoors during snowstorms. Not Wilson. He would run outside when the flakes started falling, catch them on black velvet, look at them under a microscope, and take photographs of them before they melted. His first photomicrograph of a snowflake was taken on January 15, 1885.

> Under the microscope, I found that snowflakes were miracles of beauty; and it seemed a shame that this beauty should not be seen and appreciated by others. Every crystal was a masterpiece of design and no one design was ever repeated. When a snowflake melted, that design was forever lost. Just that much beauty was gone, without leaving any record behind.[9]

The first known photographer of snowflakes, Wilson pursued his passion for more than fifty years. He amassed a collection of 5,381 photographs that was published in his magnum opus, titled *Snow Crystals*. And then he died a fitting death—a death that symbolized and epitomized his life. Wilson "Snowflake" Bentley contracted pneumonia while walking six miles through a severe snowstorm and died on December 23, 1931.

And that is how I figured out how I want to die. No, I don't want to die from pneumonia. But I do want to die doing what I love. I am determined to pursue God-ordained passions until the day I die. Life is too precious to settle for anything less.

I'm not convinced that your date of death is the date carved on your tombstone. Most people die long before that. We start dying when we have nothing worth living for. And we don't really start living until we find something worth dying for. Ironically, discovering something worth dying for is what makes life worth living.

Maybe that explains why Jesus was so full of life. He had so much—or rather so many—to die for. No one was more passionate about life than Jesus. In fact, the final chapter of His life is appropriately referred to as the Passion. And we are called to follow in His footsteps. Christ followers ought to be the most passionate people on the planet. Pursuing God-ordained passions isn't optional. It is an essential part of chasing the Wild Goose. And the adventure begins the moment we start pursuing a God-ordained passion.

RESPONSIBLE IRRESPONSIBILITY

I recently read that the average person will spend approximately half his waking hours at work. Over the course of a lifetime, that is about a hundred thousand hours on the job.[10] Based on that statistic, I have two pieces of advice. First, get yourself an ergonomic office chair. Second, and more important, don't pursue a career.

Here is the mistake so many of us make: we start out pursuing a passion and end up settling for a paycheck. So instead of making a life, all we do is make a living. And our deep-seated passions get buried beneath our day-to-day responsibilities.

Don't get me wrong. You need to take care of your responsibilities. You need to pay your bills, take out the garbage, and plan for retirement. But your greatest responsibility is pursing God-ordained passions. And if you allow less important responsibilities to displace more important ones, then you are practicing what I mentioned in the previous chapter: irresponsible responsibility.

We see that kind of mistaken attitude in a man Jesus encountered.

> [Jesus] said to another man, "Follow me."
>
> But the man replied, "Lord, first let me go and bury my father."
>
> Jesus said to him, "Let the dead bury their own dead, but you go and proclaim the kingdom of God."[11]

It seems innocent enough, doesn't it? The poor man wanted to bury his father. But Jesus saw right through the spiritual smoke screen. This man was turning a responsibility into an excuse. Burying his father was a delay tactic. He was allowing a less important responsibility to get in the way of the greatest responsibility and opportunity of his life: following Christ.

We do the same thing. We turn our responsibilities into excuses. And that is when our responsibilities actually become a form of irresponsibility. Our responsibilities become the cage that keeps us from chasing the Wild Goose. And the only way out is *responsible irresponsibility*.

Sometimes the will of God feels downright irresponsible. You are called to make a decision or take a course of action that seems to make no sense. And if you do it, the people closest to you may think you are crazy. Even Jesus' family felt that way about Him.[12] But responsible irresponsibility means refusing to allow your human responsibilities to get in the way of pursuing the passions God puts in your heart.

Enter Nehemiah.

UNQUALIFIED

A quick history lesson to put Nehemiah's passion in perspective.

In 586 BC, King Nebuchadnezzar invaded Judah, captured Jerusalem, and took many of the Jewish survivors back to Babylon. Nearly fifty years later, a Jew named Zerubbabel led the first remnant back to Jerusalem to rebuild the city. The temple was rebuilt in 516 BC, but the wall of Jerusalem was still in ruins by 445 BC. So Jerusalem was defenseless against her enemies. That is when a Jewish cupbearer, living a world away in Babylon, got a crazy idea.

> I was at the fortress of Susa. Hanani, one of my brothers, came to visit me with some other men who had just arrived from Judah. I asked them about the Jews who had returned there from captivity and about how things were going in Jerusalem.
>
> They said to me, "Things are not going well for those who returned to the province of Judah. They are in great trouble and disgrace. The wall of Jerusalem has been torn down, and the gates have been destroyed by fire."
>
> When I heard this, I sat down and wept. In fact, for days I mourned, fasted, and prayed to the God of heaven.[13]

Nehemiah had no architectural training on his transcript and no construction experience on his résumé. And as far as we know, he had never even been to Jerusalem. He was severely unqualified to pursue this passion. A cupbearer rebuilding the wall of Jerusalem is pretty laughable when you think about it. Most God-ordained passions are.

It was about as laughable as a farmer named Noah building an ark, a shepherd named David fighting a Philistine giant, or a murderer named Paul writing half of the New Testament.

When it comes to doing the will of God, God-ordained passions are far more important than any human qualification we can bring to the table. In fact, God often uses us at our point of greatest incompetence. That way He gets all the credit.

Nehemiah easily could have dismissed the desire to rebuild the wall. He could have come up with any number of excuses to stay in Babylon. Why didn't his brother do it? At least he had been to Jerusalem. Besides that, Nehemiah already had a good job. I'm not sure where cupbearer to the king ranked on the Babylonian org chart, but he was working at the White House. He didn't just have job security; there were perks and privileges attached to his position. It would have been easy for him to stay right where he was. And rebuilding the wall of Jerusalem certainly wasn't his responsibility. Or was it?

Please read prayerfully what I'm about to write. When God puts a passion in your heart, whether it be relieving starvation in Africa or educating children in the inner city or making movies with redemptive messages, that God-ordained passion becomes your responsibility. And you have a choice to make. Are you going to be irresponsibly responsible or responsibly irresponsible?

My friend Gary Haugen started an amazing human rights agency called International Justice Mission. And his story is strikingly similar to that of Nehemiah. Gary had a great job at the Department of Justice when he was loaned out to the United Nations as the chief investigator of the Rwandan genocide. Accounting for the thousands of people who were killed in that tragedy, Gary came face-to-face with human suffering on a massive scale.

Gary could have returned home and forgotten all about the suffering he had seen. Instead, Gary did the responsibly irresponsible thing to do. He personalized the problem and became part of the solution. Ten years later, IJM lawyers, investigators, and social workers are leaders in the fight to end modern slavery and oppression around the world.

I was at an IJM staff meeting not long ago. "Prayer meeting" might be a better description. Most of the employees are left-brained lawyers, but IJM doesn't run on logic alone. It runs on passion. You could tell by the way they prayed. There are plenty of law firms in DC that would pay them a fatter paycheck. But they had found a cause that was much bigger and more important than a paycheck. They are pursuing a God-ordained passion: the alleviation of human suffering.

I suppose Gary could have continued making a difference at the Department of Justice, but I think the DOJ would have become a cage for him. Gary chose to take responsibility for the passion God had put in his heart.

So I asked Gary how he had mustered the courage to hand in his resignation at DOJ and pursue this passion called IJM. And he said one of the greatest obstacles in his path was his responsibility as a husband and father. He told me that he had to confront the embarrassing possibility of failure and the need to move his entire family back in with his parents if the passion didn't pan out.

Come on, doesn't that seem a little irresponsible? Not if God is in it! That's called responsible irresponsibility.

In my experience, the will of God is difficult to discern because it often involves making a decision that seems irresponsible. You may have to quit a job or change majors or make a move. And on one level it will seem irresponsible to those who cannot see the godly motivation. But pursuing a God-ordained passion, no matter how crazy it seems, is the most responsible thing you can do.

SUCCESSFUL FAILURES

I had a professor in grad school who posed a profound question when it comes to determining God-ordained passions: "What makes you cry or pound your fist on the table?" In other words, what makes you sad? Or what makes you mad? Supernatural sadness and righteous indignation often reveal our God-ordained passions. As in the case of Nehemiah, if something causes you to weep and mourn and fast and pray for days on end, it is a good indication that God wants you to take personal responsibility and do something about it. Anything less or anything else is irresponsible responsibility.

So what makes you cry? What makes you pound your fist on the table? And let me add one more question to the mix: what makes you smile? If you want to discover your God-ordained passions, then you need to identify what makes you sad, mad, or glad. And somewhere in the sadness, madness, or gladness you will find the Wild Goose waiting for you.

God-ordained passions often break our hearts. And they can seem like an overwhelming burden to bear. But pursuing our passions is the key to living a fruitful and fulfilling life. It is the thing that wakes us up early in the morning and keeps us up late at night.

It is the thing that turns a career into a calling. It is the thing that gives us goose bumps—Wild Goose bumps. And nothing will bring you greater joy.

Frederick Buechner once wrote, "The voice we should listen to most as we choose a vocation is the voice that we might think we should listen to least, and that is the voice of our own gladness. What can we do that makes us the gladdest? I believe that if it is a thing that makes us truly glad, then it is a good thing and it is our thing."[14]

A few centuries ago there were some in the church who asked the question "Did you take pleasure in it?" to determine whether something was sinful. If it was pleasurable, it must have been wrong. What a terrible test! Even God wouldn't pass the test. His first recorded reaction in Scripture is delight in His work. Seven times the book of Genesis says, "And God saw that it was good."[15] Evidently God enjoys His job as Creator (if you can call it a job).

There is a link between goodness and gladness when we are pursuing the passions God puts in our hearts. God wants us to delight in what we do.

All of us know or have heard of people who are extremely successful and extremely unhappy. I call them successful failures. Their ladder is leaning against the wrong wall. Nehemiah could have climbed all the way up the Babylonian ladder, but he would have been disappointed when he got to the top because it wouldn't have been leaning on the wall of Jerusalem. Climbing the wrong ladder is succeeding at the wrong thing. Sure, you might make some money or get your fifteen minutes of fame. But what's the point? I would rather fail at something I love than succeed at something I don't enjoy.

THE MOMENT OF CONCEPTION

"What is it you want?" That is the question the king asked Nehemiah.[16] And it gets to the heart of passion. I'm convinced that many of our problems are by-products of the fact that most of us cannot answer that question. We don't know what we want. We've never defined our goals or values or passions, so we're out of touch with our hearts' desires. And our growing responsibilities have numbed us to the possibilities around us and the passions within us. But not Nehemiah. He knew exactly what he wanted. A passion had been conceived in his spirit. And Nehemiah had been thinking and praying about it for several months when the king posed the question.

This was the moment of truth. Nehemiah had to decide between a human responsibility and a God-ordained opportunity. Nehemiah decided to come out of the cage and chase the Wild Goose...and the adventure began. "Then I prayed to the God of heaven," he said, "and I answered the king, 'If it pleases the king and if your servant has found favor in his sight, let him send me to the city in Judah where my fathers are buried so that I can rebuild it.'"[17] That's when the passion that had been conceived began to grow in Nehemiah.

Few things are as miraculous as the moment of human conception. A sperm penetrates an egg, and all the genetic data that determine who you will become—everything from facial features to personality traits—is encoded within that single cell. And it begins a nine-month process of gestation. The mother's body starts producing hormones before she even knows she is pregnant. The baby's heart starts beating on day twenty-two. At four weeks, that single cell has grown ten thousand times larger. And around day forty-two, neurons start multiplying at the astounding rate of approximately ten thousand per second. Everything from the optic nerve to the auditory cortex to the respiratory system is being formed in the womb. What a miracle!

Sometimes I daydream about who my kids will become. How will their personalities develop? What passions will they pursue? What kind of legacy will they leave? All I know is this: I am believing God for big things! Every parent should. It is natural and normal to dream about who our children will become. But the amazing thing to me is that so much of who they ultimately become can be traced back to the moment of conception. Our destiny, in a lot of ways, is written in microscopic DNA code.

So what does that have to do with pursuing passions? Passions are conceived in much the same way. Wild Goose chases often start out as single-cell desires. Something unexplainable and inexpressible gets conceived in your spirit. Something makes you mad or sad or glad. You get Wild Goose bumps.

In the words of one psalmist, "Delight yourself in the LORD and he will give you the desires of your heart."[18] When we delight ourselves in the Lord, new desires are conceived within us. God literally downloads new desires. And those divine desires become an internal compass that guides us as we embark on a Wild Goose chase.

The exciting thing to me is that you never know how a God-ordained passion will be conceived. It might happen during a casual conversation or a mission trip. Sometimes it happens while sitting in class or reading a book. The catalyst might even be a death or divorce.

For Nehemiah, it was the news. He simply asked how things were going in Jerusalem, and his brother's answer changed the trajectory of his life. The passion to rebuild the wall of Jerusalem was conceived in his spirit. And it was followed by a gestation period. Nehemiah fasted and prayed until the passion came to full term.

If you've never identified your God-ordained passions, let me give you some simple advice. Start praying. Prayer makes us spiritually fertile. And the more we pray, the more passionate we become. Our convictions grow stronger, and our dreams grow bigger.

It's no coincidence that there are eight references to prayer in Nehemiah's memoir. Nehemiah prayed like it depended on God. And that is half of pursuing your passions. The other half is working like it depends on you. Or maybe I should say it this way: you need to start praying...and then you need to quit praying and start doing something about it.

TIME TO QUIT PRAYING

Several years ago I was part of a small group with a friend who was working with InterVarsity Christian Fellowship at Georgetown University. As we shared prayer requests at the end of one of our meetings, my friend said their ministry needed a computer and I said I'd pray for him. I started praying that God would provide a computer, and then I felt as if God interrupted me. It's hard to describe the tone I heard from God. It was stern but not unkind. It was as if the Holy Spirit whispered these words to my spirit: *Why are you asking Me? You're the one with the extra computer!*

So I quit praying midsentence and decided to do something about it. I told my friend I had a computer that I wanted to give him. And I became the answer to my own prayer. Why ask God to do something for us when it is within our power to do something about it ourselves?

There are some things you *don't* need to pray about. You don't need to pray about whether you should love your neighbor. You don't need to pray about whether you should give generously or serve sacrificially. You don't need to pray about whether you should bless someone when it is within your power to do so. God has already spoken. What you need to do is quit praying and start acting.

Fill out the application.

Make the call.

Pack the U-Haul.

Write the check.

Set up the appointment.

Have the conversation.

Make the move.

I've been challenged by the action-oriented approach to Scripture proposed by Peter Marshall, former chaplain of the United States Senate.

I wonder what would happen if we all agreed to read one of the Gospels until we came to a place that told us to do something, then went out to do it, and only after we had done it, began reading again? There are aspects of the Gospel that are puzzling and difficult to understand. But our problems are not centered around the things we don't understand, but rather in the things we do understand, the things we could not possibly misunderstand. Our problem is not so much that we don't know what we should do. We know perfectly well, but we don't want to do it.[19]

Please don't misinterpret what I'm trying to say. Pray about everything. Then pray some more. But at some point, you need to quit praying and start acting.

One of the great mistakes we make is asking God to do for us what God wants us to do for Him. We confuse portfolios. For example, we try to convict the people around us of sin. But that is the Holy Spirit's responsibility, not ours. And when we play God, we not only do a poor job at it, but it is always counterproductive. In the same sense, God won't do for us what we can do for ourselves. And that is where so many of us get stuck spiritually.

I recently received an e-mail from an NCCer named Becky who has pursued a God-ordained passion halfway around the world.

I went to India to work with women and children who were trafficked into sex slavery. Most of these women were Nepalese and ended up working as forced prostitutes in India's infamous red-light districts. Their children were literally born into brothels and knew nothing of life except violence, rape, and hunger. Although I wasn't able to rescue the women from their situation, I was able to offer hope and empowerment for the survivors and children. I led dance therapy sessions, helping to reconnect the survivors to their bodies and allowing them to see themselves as beautiful creations of God.

The area we were working in was devastatingly poor,

malaria infested, and as an antitrafficking activist, I was
in danger from the traffickers and brothel owners. So my
parents pleaded with me to leave. But I couldn't stay away.
I could see God in each of their bloodshot, traumatized,
beautiful eyes, begging me to touch, to comfort, to hug,
and ultimately to love them.

If Christians believe that God is in every person, why
don't we act like that? Why do we turn our eyes from the
poor, the widows, the orphans, and the prostitutes? Although
prayer is necessary and helps bring comfort, it's not enough
to truly alleviate suffering. God didn't send His Son to pray
for us but rather to act for us. The only thing that upsets me
more than downright evil acts are people who allow injustice
to happen with their inaction. Jesus transformed God's message into action, and it should be our mission to devote our
lives to similar action.

When *Christianity* turns into a noun, it becomes a turnoff.
Christianity was always intended to be a verb. And, more specifically,
an action verb. The title of the book of Acts says it all, doesn't it? It's
not the book of *Ideas* or *Theories* or *Words*. It's the book of *Acts*. If
the twenty-first-century church said less and did more, maybe we
would have the same kind of impact the first-century church did.

Some of us live as if we expect to hear God say, "Well *thought*,
good and faithful servant!" or "Well *said*, good and faithful servant!"
God isn't going to say either of those things. There is only one com-
mendation, and it is the by-product of pursing God-ordained passions: "Well *done*, good and faithful servant!"[20]

WET FEET

Not long ago I had breakfast with a friend who works for the Willow Creek Association based out of the Chicago area. Paul was in town for an annual prayer breakfast at the White House, and I asked him how he got invited. All right, I admit it. I was a little jealous!

Paul told me that he had a feeling that he needed to be at that prayer breakfast, but he wasn't sure why or how to get himself invited. He wasn't trying to manipulate or manufacture something; he just felt that God wanted him there.

Paul happened to know someone with White House connections, so he asked a friend if he could get him on the invitee list. His connection said he'd do what he could, but it was a pretty short list. Paul checked in with his friend every few weeks—six weeks out, four weeks out, two weeks out, two days out. Nothing!

The day before the event, Paul was checking e-mail every five minutes. No invitation. But he couldn't get rid of the unexplainable impression that he needed to be there. So at 4:30 p.m., on the day before the event, he called an airline to see if he could get a last-minute ticket. There was one more flight with one more seat that departed O'Hare International Airport at 7:30 p.m. So Paul called his wife and said, "Talk me out of it." She didn't talk him out of it. In fact, she packed his suitcase and met him at the airport with it. It felt like a Wild Goose chase hopping a flight without an invitation, but that is exactly what Paul did.

When he landed in DC, he found a hotel with Wi-Fi and immediately checked his e-mail. The e-mail invitation never came, so he hopped a flight back to Chicago the next morning and decided never to do anything like that again.

I'm just kidding. It could have ended that way, but it didn't.

While he was airborne to DC, Paul received an invitation, which was waiting in his e-mail in-box when he landed. And he realized that if he hadn't hopped the last flight that night, he never would have made the prayer breakfast, because the earliest morning flights out of Chicago would have arrived too late to make the event.

Now here is the backstory. The morning before the breakfast, Paul used the infamous flip-open-your-Bible-and-start-reading-wherever-it-lands Bible-study method. I'm not recommending that method as a consistent approach to Bible study, but sometimes it works in strange and mysterious ways. Anyway, Paul's finger happened to land in the part of the book of Joshua where the Israelites are on the verge of entering the Promised Land and God tells the priests to take a few steps into the river.[21]

I've always been intrigued by that command because if I were one of the priests, I would be thinking the opposite. *God, why don't You part the water, and* then *I'll step into the river? That way my feet won't get wet.* But I think this was a spiritual test. I think God wanted to see if the priests had enough faith to get their feet wet. And if they were willing to take that first step of faith, then He would miraculously part the Jordan River.

At four thirty in the afternoon, Paul remembered the passage he had read that morning and felt as if God were telling him to step into the river and get his feet wet by purchasing a plane ticket to DC. And the rest is His-story.

Discerning the will of God is not an exact science. I don't have any seven-step formulas for you. And I want you to know that I've missed it more than once. But I do know that God will use a combination of the Holy Spirit and Holy Scripture to guide us. If we open His Word, God will open His mouth and speak to us through it. And when the Word of God is conceived in our spirits, we've got to act on it. We need to quit praying and get our feet wet.

You know why some of us have never seen God part a river? Because our feet are still firmly planted on dry ground. We're waiting on God while God is waiting on us!

SIGNS FOLLOWING

Most of us want God to provide miraculous signs *before* we come out of the cage. We want God to part the river before we get our feet wet. Why? So our faith doesn't require any faith! Don't get me wrong. Sometimes God will provide a miraculous sign that will give you just enough faith to take the first step in the pursuit of your passion. But more often than not, faith doesn't follow signs. *Signs follow faith.* It is the biblical pattern.

The book of Mark concludes this way: "They went forth, and preached every where, the Lord working with them, and confirming the word with signs following."[22] If you're going to chase the Wild Goose, you need to come to terms with the last two words of Mark's gospel: "signs following."

In my experience, signs follow decisions. The way you overcome spiritual inertia and produce spiritual momentum is by making tough decisions. And the tougher the decision, the more potential momentum it will produce. The primary reason most of us don't see God moving is simply because we aren't moving. If you want to see God move, you need to make a move!

I learned this lesson in dramatic fashion during our first year at National Community Church. We had been praying for a drummer to join our worship team for months, but I felt like I needed to put some feet on my faith, so I went out and bought a four-hundred-dollar drum set. It was a *Field of Dreams* moment: if you buy it, they will come. I bought the drum set on a Thursday. Our first drummer showed up the next Sunday. And he was good. He was actually part of the United States Marine Drum and Bugle Corps.

Rock and roll.

I cannot promise that signs will follow your faith in three minutes or three hours or three days. But when you take a step of faith, signs will follow. God will sanctify your expectations, and you will begin to live your life with holy anticipation. You won't be able to wait to see what God is going to do next.

Nehemiah didn't wait for a sign. He had the courage to put his job on the line. And when he did, God confirmed the passion with signs following. The king didn't just write him a nice reference; the king wrote him a blank check.

> I also said to him, "If it pleases the king, may I have letters to the governors of Trans-Euphrates, so that they will provide me safe-conduct until I arrive in Judah? And may I have a letter to Asaph, keeper of the king's forest, so he will give me timber to make beams for the gates of the citadel by the temple and for the city wall and for the residence I will occupy?"

And because the gracious hand of my God was upon me,
the king granted my requests. So I went to the governors of
Trans-Euphrates and gave them the king's letters. The king
had also sent army officers and cavalry with me.[23]

There are moments in life when our passions and the purposes
of God converge in what I call *supernatural synchronicities*. These are
the moments when we come alive. These are the moments when the
sovereignty of God overshadows our incompetencies. And these are
the moments when our success can be attributed to only one thing:
the favor of God. God does something for us that we could never do
for ourselves.

This was that kind of moment for Nehemiah. Sure, Nehemiah
had done some serious strategizing. He knew exactly what to ask for,
didn't he? But God's fingerprints were all over this situation. The
king didn't just give him permission to rebuild the wall. He didn't
just give him references and resources. He sent his army with
Nehemiah. And it all traced back to this: Nehemiah prayed for favor
and God granted it.

I pray for favor all the time. In fact, I pray for favor more than I
pray for anything else. I pray for the favor of God on my children. I
pray for the favor of God on my own life. And I pray for the favor
of God on National Community Church. And it is the favor of God
that gives me a sense of destiny. I know that God can intervene at
any moment and turn it into a defining moment. That is what happened on August 12, 2001.

Growth didn't come easy for National Community Church our
first few years. Then, on that August date, the *Washington Post* ran an

article on NCC. I thought it would be buried in the religion section, but instead it landed on the front page of the Sunday edition. In the weeks that followed, hundreds of first-time visitors walked through our front doors, and we experienced our first exponential growth spurt.

Listen, any one of us can make the news. Just do something stupid. But good press is the favor of God. And I'm convinced that God did something for our church we never could have done for ourselves. That article put us on the map in the DC area.

Can I share a growing desire in my life? I don't want to do things I am capable of doing. Why? Because then I can take credit for them. I want to see God do things in me and through me that I am absolutely incapable of so I can't possibly take credit for them.

The Best Cupbearer

Every week I have the privilege of preaching to thousands of people in person and via podcast, and I'm grateful for the opportunity to influence them. But let me tell you how I got my start. When God conceived the passion to preach in me, I started speaking at homeless shelters and nursing homes. I was the John Wesley of the nursing-home circuit. And there was nothing glamorous about it. During one of my nursing-home sermons, an octogenarian suffering from dementia stood up in the middle of my message and started undressing while yelling at the top of her lungs, "Get him out of here! Get him out of here!" Not much fazes you after that.

During college I attended a church with an average attendance of twelve people. But that is where I cut my teeth preaching. By the way, the church only had seven pews. I often wondered about the person who built that church. What vision! *Someday this thing may grow so big we'll fill seven whole pews.* Of course, my early sermons didn't help the cause!

I know I'm making light of those opportunities now, but back in the day I took them as seriously as sin. I prepared for each of those messages as if it were the most important one I'd ever preach. And I did it because I believed that if I was faithful in the little things, God would give me bigger things to do. If I made the most of the mustard-seed opportunities, God would expand my sphere of influence.

Maybe you feel a little like Nehemiah. Your passion is Jerusalem, yet you're stuck a thousand miles due east in Babylon. You have no idea how to get from where you are to where you want to be. You don't like your job. You don't like your boss. Or you don't like your prospects. And the passion has been sucked out of your spirit.

I love pastoring and writing, but I certainly don't want to give the impression that I jump out of bed every morning ready to take on the world. For the record, I generally hit my snooze button two or three times. I often wake up with a stiff back. And the first thing I do every day is take our dog for a walk and pick up his poop. There is nothing glorious or glamorous about that.

And over the years I've had plenty of jobs that were nothing more than a paycheck. My first job in high school was at a gas station. I hated wearing that ugly brown uniform, especially when friends stopped by. One summer during college I worked as a ditch digger, which might explain the stiff back. And when I started pastoring NCC, I had to work two jobs just to make ends meet.

I think all of us have been stuck in Babylon. So what do you do when you're in those situations or seasons? Here is the best advice I can offer: *be the best cupbearer you can be*. This is where the adventure begins.

Don't whine. Don't complain. And don't check out. Make the most of the situation. Do little things like they are big things. Keep a good attitude. And faithfully carry out your current obligations. If your job isn't exciting, then bring some excitement to the job. One of the greatest acts of worship is keeping a good attitude in a bad situation. And doing a good job at a bad job honors God. It will also open doors of opportunity down the road. It did for Nehemiah.

Based on the biblical record, I think it's fair to assume that Nehemiah had an upbeat attitude. He brought positive energy to his job day in and day out. How do I know that? Because the king noticed a change in Nehemiah's demeanor. The opportunity of a lifetime was set up by his everyday attitude. "I had not been sad in his presence before; so the king asked me, 'Why does your face look so sad when you are not ill? This can be nothing but sadness of heart.' "[24]

Nehemiah had an ordinary job, testing food, waiting tables, and washing dishes. But he did the best he could with what he had where he was. In my book that is success. Nehemiah was successful long before he rebuilt the wall of Jerusalem. And I've found that if you are faithful in Babylon, God will often bless you a thousand miles away.

"FIND YOUR OWN CALCUTTA"

In some ways, Nehemiah seems like an overnight success. He rebuilt the wall of Jerusalem in fifty-two days flat. But the passion was internalized months before it was verbalized.[25] The journey to Jerusalem must have taken several months. And Nehemiah experienced considerable opposition along the way from a couple of ancient thugs named Sanballat and Tobiah.

Sometimes when we read the stories of biblical characters, we underestimate how long it took for them to accomplish what they accomplished. And we underestimate how hard it was. We can read their stories in a matter of minutes, so we tend to overlook the fact that, in most instances, their passions were unpursued or unfulfilled for years on end. In my experience, the Wild Goose doesn't take shortcuts. He loves leading us down the scenic route because that is where we learn our most valuable lessons.

I'm not sure where you are in your Wild Goose chase. Maybe you feel like you're trapped in a dead-end job. Maybe your passions are buried beneath your responsibilities. Or maybe you feel like you'll waste too many credits if you change majors now. I don't know what is keeping you from pursuing your God-ordained passions, but I do know that if you have the courage to come out of the cage, it will change your life.

Agnes Gonxha Bojaxhiu felt called to ministry when she was a teenager. She did her ministerial training in Ireland and India. And one day she approached her superiors with a God-ordained passion. She said, "I have three pennies and a dream from God to build an orphanage."

Her superiors said, "You can't build an orphanage with three pennies. With three pennies you can't do anything."

Agnes smiled and said, "I know. But with God and three pennies I can do anything."[26]

For fifty years Agnes worked among the poor in the slums of Calcutta, India. In 1979 the woman we know as Mother Teresa won the Nobel Peace Prize. Listen, it is a long way from three pennies to a Nobel Peace Prize. And my question is, how did a woman with so little do so much? The answer is simple. Never underestimate someone who has the courage to come out of the cage and pursue a God-ordained passion.

Toward the end of her ministry, Mother Teresa was often asked by her admirers how they could make a difference with their lives the way she had with hers. Mother Teresa's oft-repeated response was four words long: "Find your own Calcutta."

Now let me bring it a little closer to home, because Calcutta seems like half a world away.

A few years ago I performed a funeral for a Senate staffer who attended NCC. Jayona never held a position of power. She was an administrative assistant in charge of constituent correspondence—an entry-level position on Capitol Hill. Jayona opened mail for fourteen years. But she was the best constituent correspondent she could be. She also sewed buttons for colleagues, showed interns the ropes, and baked a mean batch of chocolate-chip cookies.

I'll never forget her memorial service. It was held in the Caucus Room in the Russell Senate Office Building. Some of the most important people have attended some of the most important hearings in our nation's history in that room. The service was packed with people coming to pay their respects, and I had the opportunity to tell them that Jayona would want them to have what she had—a personal relationship with Jesus Christ. I'm guessing lots of colleagues and a few members of Congress heard a clear presentation of the gospel for the first time in their lives that day. And it was all set up by a woman who found her Calcutta on Capitol Hill.

You don't need wealth or position or power to make a difference. You just need to do the best you can with what you have where you are. And if you are faithful in Babylon, God will bless you in Jerusalem.

Be the best cupbearer you can be!

That's responsible irresponsibility. That's pursuing passion.

YOUR CHASE

- ❈ Which describes you better: irresponsibly responsible or responsibly irresponsible? Why is that?
- ❈ What makes you sad or mad or glad? In other words, what passions has God given to you?
- ❈ What have you been praying about lately that God wants you to quit praying about? And what does God want you to do instead?
- ❈ God asked the priests carrying the ark to step into the river before He dammed it up. How do you need to get your feet wet in pursuing your God-given passions?
- ❈ What little things do you need to be doing now that will prepare you for the big things God wants to do down the road?

CHAPTER 3

DICTATORSHIP OF THE ORDINARY

Coming Out of the Cage of Routine

Earth's crammed with heaven,
And every common bush afire with God;
But only he who sees takes off his shoes;
The rest sit round it and pluck blackberries.

—ELIZABETH BARRETT BROWNING

Right now you have no sensation of motion. I'm guessing you're sitting still as you read *Wild Goose Chase*. But the reality is that you are sitting on a planet that is spinning around its axis at approximately one thousand miles per hour. Planet earth will make one full rotation in the next twenty-four hours. Not only that, but you are also hurtling through space at approximately sixty-seven thousand miles per hour. And you didn't have any big plans for today! Before the day is done, you will have traveled 1.3 million miles in your annual trek around the sun.

Now let me ask you a question. When was the last time you thanked God for keeping us in orbit? I'm guessing never. *Lord, thanks for keeping us in orbit. And I was a little nervous about making the full rotation around our axis today, but You did it again.* Most of us don't pray that way. But isn't it a little ironic that we have a hard time believing God for the little stuff while we take the big stuff for granted. Come on, if God can keep the planets in orbit, don't you think He can reorder your life when you feel like it's spinning out of control?

Keeping the planets in orbit is a perpetual miracle of unparalleled proportions. So why aren't we overwhelmed with awe over our annual orbit? Why don't we ceaselessly praise God for our spinning globe? The reason is simple: *we take constants for granted.* And that is the problem with God, if I may say it that way. God is the ultimate constant. He is unconditionally loving. He is omnipotently powerful. And He is eternally faithful. God is so good at what God does that we tend to take Him for granted.

Thomas Carlyle, the nineteenth-century Scottish essayist, once imagined a man who had lived his entire life in a cave stepping outside for the first time and witnessing the sunrise. Carlyle said that the cave man would watch with rapt astonishment the sight we daily witness with indifference.

In the words of G. K. Chesterton, "Grown-up people are not strong enough to exult in monotony. Is it possible God says every morning, 'Do it again' to the sun; and every evening, 'Do it again' to the moon? The repetition in nature may not be a mere recurrence; it may be a theatrical encore."

That seems to be what Psalm 29 suggests: "Bravo, GOD, bravo! Gods and all angels shout, 'Encore!' "[27]

INATTENTIONAL BLINDNESS

When was the last time you, as an act of worship, watched the sunrise? or a lunar eclipse? or a snowfall?

A few years ago I met an exchange student from India who had never seen snow. So when meteorologists issued a winter storm warning for the DC area, he got excited. In fact, he set his alarm for three o'clock in the morning because he didn't want to miss the first flakes falling. He went outside all by himself and made snow angels. The funny thing is that he didn't wear a jacket or gloves. He said he didn't realize snow is cold.

There is nothing like experiencing something for the first time. It's unforgettable, isn't it? Time slows to a standstill, and we become hypersensitive to the stimuli around us. Those moments are engraved in our memories. But then we get back into the routine of life, and the cataracts of the habitual cloud our vision.

I know people who say they have never experienced a miracle. But with all due respect, I beg to differ. We are surrounded by miracles. They are all around us all the time. We just take them for granted.

Our minds are wired in such a way that when a new stimulus is introduced into our environment we become intensely aware of it. But over time we adapt to the sights, sounds, and smells that constantly surround us. Eventually awareness fades, and the constants in our environment become invisible. Psychologists call this process *inattentional blindness*. It happens with sunrises. And snow. And life in general.

It is so easy to lose the joy of living, isn't it? Few things compare to the joy experienced by a bride and groom on their wedding day, but take romance out of the equation, and the relationship becomes routine. The birth of a child is an awe-inspiring miracle, but start changing dirty diapers in the middle of the night, and some of the joy goes away. And most of us were joyful when we landed our job, but too many people end up living for the weekend.

What happens is this: the sacred becomes routine. And we not only forfeit spiritual adventure but we also start losing the joy of our salvation. Chasing the Wild Goose is the way to get it back. But that means coming out of the cage of the routine. We need to change our routine, take some risks, and try new things. And if we do, we will find ourselves coming alive again.

When we moved to Washington DC, my first job was directing a parachurch organization. And it was a comfortable routine. So was living in the suburbs. But that wasn't what God had for us. My Wild Goose chase required a risk in the form of National Community Church. And to be perfectly honest, moving into the city was out of my comfort zone at first. But over the years I've come to appreciate a unique dimension of the Holy Spirit's personality. Jesus called him the Counselor.[28] He comforts the afflicted. But like a good counselor, He also afflicts the comfortable. And I came to a place in my life where I was uncomfortable with my level of comfort.

Where have you gotten too comfortable as a Christ follower?

Where has life become too routine? What have you turned a blind eye to? I don't know where you need to be afflicted, but I do know this: if you let routine rule your life, you'll never get where the Wild Goose wants you to go.

Enter Moses.

THE BURNING BUSH

Tending sheep. Can you imagine a more routine existence? Moses must have felt like he had been put out to pasture. He once dreamed of delivering the people of Israel out of captivity. But that dream died when he killed an Egyptian taskmaster and fled the country as a fugitive. Moses spent the next forty years on the backside of the desert shearing sheep. And I have a feeling that Moses got up this particular morning, put on his sandals and picked up his staff, and figured it would be an ordinary day just like the day before…and the day before the day before…and the day before that. But you never know when or where the Wild Goose is going to invade the routine of your life.

> Moses was tending the flock of Jethro his father-in-law, the priest of Midian, and he led the flock to the far side of the desert and came to Horeb, the mountain of God. There the angel of the LORD appeared to him in flames of fire from within a bush. Moses saw that though the bush was on fire it did not burn up. So Moses thought, "I will go over and see this strange sight—why the bush does not burn up."
>
> When the LORD saw that he had gone over to look, God called to him from within the bush, "Moses! Moses!"

And Moses said, "Here I am."

"Do not come any closer," God said. "Take off your sandals, for the place where you are standing is holy ground."[29]

Have you ever experienced an epiphany—a moment when God
unexpectedly and unforgettably invaded the monotony of your life?
A few years ago I was on a tour bus driving through the Andes
Mountains from Guayaquil to Cuenca, Ecuador. We couldn't see the
mountain peaks because of cloud cover, but we kept climbing the
winding mountain road. Eventually we drove through the ceiling of
clouds, and they turned into a celestial carpet. What a view from
twelve thousand feet! It was the closest I've ever come to feeling like
I was on top of the world. And I was so overcome by the majesty of
those mountain peaks that I started clapping. It just seemed like the
Creator deserved a round of applause.

The Celtic Christians referred to these kinds of moments—
moments when heaven and earth seem to touch—as *thin places*. Natural and supernatural worlds collide. Creation meets Creator. Sin
meets grace. Routine meets the Wild Goose.

This was one of those moments and one of those places for
Moses. God showed up. And an ordinary place—a bush on the
backside of the desert—became holy ground. That seems to be the
way the Holy Spirit works, doesn't it? He is predictably unpredictable. He loves to show up in wild places at wild times.

Jewish scholars used to debate why God appeared to Moses in a
burning bush. A thunderclap or lightning bolt would have been
more impressive. And why the far side of the desert? They concluded
that God appeared to Moses in a burning bush to show that no place

is devoid of God's presence, not even a bush on the backside of the desert. One name for God in rabbinical literature is The Place.[30] God is here, there, and everywhere. So it doesn't matter where you are. You can be sitting in rush-hour traffic, working at your desk, or lying on your sofa. God can show up anytime, anyplace!

I think this is one of those stories in which the obvious can elude us. The holy ground wasn't the Promised Land. It was right where Moses was standing. Don't wait to worship God till you get to the Promised Land; you've got to worship along the way. *This* is holy ground. *This* is a holy moment. Take off your sandals.

When I was nineteen years old, our family vacationed in Alexandria, Minnesota, just as we had every summer since I was born. I had just finished my freshman year at the University of Chicago and had declared a major: pre-law. But I wasn't sure that was what I really wanted to do or what God wanted me to do. So I asked God a dangerous question: "What do You want me to do with my life?" By the way, the only thing more dangerous than asking that question is not asking that question.

If you ask God that question with a willingness to do whatever He says, you'd better be prepared for God to disrupt the routine of your life. That question began what I retroactively call my "summer of seeking." And it culminated on the last day of vacation during the last week of summer break. I broke the vacation routine of sleeping in and got up early to go on a prayer walk. I walked down some dirt roads and took a shortcut through a cow pasture, and it was there that I heard the inaudible yet unmistakable voice of God.

I don't want to paint the scene as more dramatic than it really was. There were no angelic choirs. No skywriting planes. But I knew in my spirit that God was calling me into full-time ministry. I didn't know the specifics. In fact, the when, where, and how would remain a mystery for several years. But that cow pasture was a "thin place" for me.

Several years ago I took a pilgrimage back to that cow pasture, and I hired a photographer to take some pictures. One of them sits behind the desk in my office. Why? Because I have tough days just like everybody else, and I need a burning bush to remind me of why I'm doing what I'm doing. That picture hangs in my office as an altar to God.

Have you ever noticed how often people in the Old Testament built altars? It seems like they were building them all over the place all the time. Why? Because we have a natural tendency to remember what we should forget and forget what we should remember. Altars help us remember what God doesn't want us to forget. They give us a sacred place to go back to.

So why did we stop building altars? I honestly wonder if our lives seem more routine than they really are simply because we don't have any altars dotting the landscape. I wonder if many of us feel spiritually lost because we don't have any milestones that help us find our way back to God. We need altars that renew our faith by reminding us of the faithfulness of God. And every once in a while, we need to go back to those sacred places to repent of our sin, renew our covenant with God, and celebrate what God has done.

I wonder if Peter ever rowed out to that spot on the Sea of Galilee where he walked on water. Did Zacchaeus ever take his grandchildren back to climb the sycamore tree where he caught his first glimpse of Jesus? Did Lazarus ever revisit the tomb where he was buried for four days? Did Paul ever ride out to the mile marker on the road to Damascus where God knocked him off his high horse? Did Abraham ever take Isaac back to Mount Moriah, where God provided a ram in the thicket? And I wonder if Moses ever returned to the burning bush, took off his sandals, and thanked God for interrupting the forty-year routine of his life by giving him a second chance to make a difference.

THE GEOGRAPHY OF SPIRITUALITY

I think we underestimate the interconnection between geography and spirituality. And part of the reason is that we worship God in man made buildings that keep us insulated from the elements. We sit in the same padded pew, week in and week out, listening to stories about Jesus calming the wind and the waves. The disciples had a totally different experience. They were in the boat on the lake when the skies grew dark and hurricane winds started to blow.[31] They walked beaches, climbed mountains, and trekked across the wilderness with Jesus. Their experience was four-dimensional, while ours is one-dimensional. So when we read the Bible, we tend to focus on theology, overlooking the meteorology, the psychology, and even the geology that shape the stories we read.

Remember when Jesus took Peter, James, and John up the Mount of Transfiguration? We don't give the elevation issue a second thought, right? But Scripture specifically says it was a *high* mountain.[32] This was no bunny hill. So what? Well, here's what I know about mountains: the higher they are, the harder they are to climb. I can imagine Peter, James, and John scrambling to keep up with

Jesus and beat each other to the top. And when they finally got to the top of that mountain, they had to be exhausted from the climb. But if you've ever scaled a mountain peak, you know that the view from the top is worth every ounce of energy you expended to get there.

What Peter, James, and John experienced on that mountain forever changed the way they saw Jesus. Certainly the metamorphosis Jesus underwent was the catalyst. And the appearance of Moses and Elijah left them speechless. But is it fair to say that the place where it happened was part of the equation? Was climbing a high mountain a strategic move on Jesus' part? I think it was. When God wants us to experience a change in perspective, He often does it via a change in scenery. So Jesus took the three disciples to a new place— a high place, a place that was far removed from civilization.

Here's the bottom line: where you are geographically affects where you are spiritually. A few years ago I came up with a simple formula:

change of place + change of pace = change of perspective

Why are retreats and mission trips such powerful catalysts in our lives? Part of the reason is the change in latitude and longitude. New places open us up to new experiences. They get us out of our routine and help us see God with new eyes.

If you're in a spiritual slump, let me give you a prescription: go on a mission trip.[33] There is no better or sure way of coming out of the cage of routine. It's a cure-all.

I recently got an e-mail from an NCCer who could have exchanged her award miles for a nice little Caribbean getaway. But she felt prompted by God to use her miles to fly to India and offer her nursing skills at a medical clinic. Ana Luisa spent a month at an understaffed and underequipped medical clinic. And she didn't just treat the people there as a nurse would; she loved them as a Christ follower does. One of her patients was a little baby girl born with spina bifida and full paralysis in both legs.

> In many parts of India, baby boys are significantly preferred over girls, so you can imagine the mood among the family when they learned their little girl was born with such serious disabilities. The hospital staff was actually worried that the parents would abandon the baby in the middle of the night or take her home and kill her. In the first few days following her birth, the parents would not touch her, feed her, or talk to her. The grandmother was the only one that demonstrated any sort of warmth toward the baby. Again, I used my novice nursing skills as an excuse to go visit the baby every day.
>
> At first the feeling in the room of about six family members made me feel like chickening out, but by God's power I boldly asked the father if I could pray over the child. I was surprised that he said yes. I prayed over the baby out loud, and despite the language barrier, the whole family heard the name of Jesus repeatedly. I talked to the baby, stroked her, and whispered to her that Jesus loves her. About the fourth day the father asked me to name her! Wow! After prayerful thought, I chose the name Gloria. They accepted it, and the father even said it was nice. I continue to pray for a miracle and am excited to see what the Lord does.

I don't believe in coincidence. I believe in providence. I believe in a sovereign God who sets up divine appointments half a world away. He can use any one of us to touch anyone else in the world. And if you listen to the still, small voice and follow the lead of the Wild Goose, you never know where it will lead. But God will write His-story through your life!

It is easy to become self-absorbed, isn't it? I don't doubt that you have your fair share of problems. I know I have mine. But there is nothing like a mission trip to put them in perspective.

THE FOURTH COMMANDMENT

If you want to come out of the cage of routine, change of place is half of the equation. The other half is change of pace.

Last year I discovered the importance of pacing when running my first triathlon. I did all my training for the swim leg of the race in a pool. And my times were fantastic. But the Atlantic Ocean is no pool. I was confident going into the race. And so on the opening swim leg, I sprinted from the beach to the first buoy. I wanted to be at the front of the pack so I didn't have to embarrass everybody by swimming past them. That's just the kind of guy I am.

Well, let's just say that the ocean ate my lunch! Or more accurately, I drank the ocean. It's amazing what a couple gallons of salt water will do to your stomach. Lora said I looked like a dazed boxer when I finally hit the beach. She was being kind. I started so fast that I couldn't catch my breath the rest of the swim. I'm embarrassed to say that I ended up doing the backstroke instead of freestyle for much of the swim leg. And I learned an important lesson: how you start is not nearly as important as how you finish. And pacing is the key.

Someone recently asked me the greatest challenge I'm facing in my life right now. The answer was easy: margin. With pastoring, parenting, writing, and speaking, I don't have much margin in my life. And National Community Church isn't launching new locations because we need one more thing to do! Honestly, the larger the church gets, the less equal to the task I feel. It seems like I have to run faster and faster just to stay in the same place.

I know from experience that you can do the work of God at a pace that destroys the work of God in you. And I want to do ministry at a sustainable pace. But can I make a confession? One of my greatest challenges is keeping the fourth commandment. I have a tough time taking a Sabbath. In fact, last year I had to make a New Year's resolution not to check work-related e-mail on my day off. I also resolved to use all my vacation days. I feel like I owe it to my family, and I owe it to God.

Have you ever wondered why God would institute a Sabbath? Doesn't it seem like we could accomplish more for His cause if we worked seven days a week? So why did God stop working on the seventh day? It certainly wasn't because He needed a break. Here's my take. The Sabbath is a weekly reminder that we don't keep the planets in orbit; He does. But you'd never know it by our frenetic efforts to get to the bottom of our to-do lists. You know what you really need? A stop-doing list!

I have come to this conclusion: I don't want to be good at lots of things; I want to be great at a few things. I would rather pour my heart, soul, mind, and strength into a few endeavors than do lots of things halfway. And I've had to reprioritize my passions.

A few years ago I poured significant time and money into a start-up business. We were first movers in a unique market niche. But I ended up realizing that if I didn't kill the business, the business was going to kill me. I knew I couldn't keep up the pace. And as I assessed my gifts and callings, I knew that pastoring and writing were my primary God-ordained passions. Even if the business venture were successful, it would short-circuit what God wanted to do in me and through me.

What do you need to give up? Where do you need to slow down? What changes do you need to make in your life to give God margin to work in?

The Sabbath is one way we let go and let God. It's a healthy change of pace. It creates a holy margin in our lives. And it keeps what is sacred from becoming routine.

In his book *Anam Cara,* John O'Donohue tells a story about a European explorer in Africa who hired some native Africans to help carry his equipment through the jungle. They didn't stop for three days. At the end of the third day, the hired hands stopped and refused to move on. The explorer asked why, and one of the African natives said, "We have moved too quickly to reach here; now we need to wait to give our spirits a chance to catch up with us."

The word *Sabbath* means "to catch one's breath." A weekly Sabbath is the way our spirits catch up with our bodies. And if we don't slow down, we eventually hit the point of diminishing returns, where more is less and less is more. It's counterintuitive, but the way you speed up is by slowing down.

A Wild Goose chase isn't a mad dash. It's more of a triathlon. And pacing yourself for the journey is critical. Yes, there will be moments when it seems next to impossible to keep in step with the long strides of the Spirit. But I think it's even more difficult, for those of us with Type-A personalities, to slow down when God wants us to be still.

Why did God tell Moses to take off his sandals? I think it was God's way of saying, "Be still, and know that I am God."[34]

MINISTRY HAPPENS

When we don't pace ourselves, we tend to miss divine appointments right and left. In fact, they seem like human interruptions. We get so consumed with trying to get where we think God wants us to go that we put on spiritual blinders and miss the Goose trails He wants to take us down. The way you chase the Wild Goose isn't by going faster and faster. The key is slowing down your pace, taking off your sandals, and experiencing God right here, right now.

A few years ago, two Princeton University psychologists did an experiment that was inspired by a Bible story.[35] Jesus told a story about a traveler who was mugged and left for dead on the side of the road between Jerusalem and Jericho. A priest and a Levite (people who fit the religious profile in Jesus' culture) walked by on the other side of the street. The only one to stop and help was a Samaritan.

John Darley and Daniel Batson decided to replicate the story of the good Samaritan with seminary students. A few variables were introduced. The seminarians were interviewed and asked why they wanted to go into ministry. There were a variety of responses, but the vast majority said they went into ministry to help people. Then they were asked to prepare a short sermon—half of them on the story of the good Samaritan and the other half on other topics. Finally they were told to go over to a building on campus to present their sermons.

Along the way, the researchers had strategically positioned an actor in an alley to play the part of the man who was mugged in Jesus' story. He was slumped over and groaning loud enough for passersby to hear.

The researchers hypothesized that those who said they went into ministry to help people and those who had just prepared the sermon on the good Samaritan would be the most likely to stop and help. But that wasn't the case. And the reason is the final variable introduced by the researchers. Just before the seminarians left to give their sermon, the researcher looked at his watch and said one of two things. To some seminarians, the researcher said, "You're late. They were expecting you a few minutes ago. You better hurry." To others, the researcher said, "You're early. They aren't expecting you for a few minutes, but why don't you start heading over there?"

Interested in the results? Only 10 percent of the seminary students who were in a hurry stopped to help, while 63 percent of those who weren't in a hurry stopped to help. In several cases, a seminary student going to give his talk on the parable of the good Samaritan literally stepped over the victim as he hurried on his way!

Darley and Batson concluded that it didn't matter whether someone wanted to help people or whether someone had just read and was preparing to preach on the parable of the good Samaritan. The only thing that mattered was whether or not they were in a hurry. They concluded, "The words, 'You're late,' had the effect of making someone who was ordinarily compassionate into someone who was indifferent to suffering."[36]

Hurry kills everything from compassion to creativity. And when you're in a hurry, you don't have time to get out of your routine, do you? No room for Spirit-led spontaneity. No time for Wild Goose chases. Here is the great irony: the priest and the Levite were probably on their way to the temple. They were so busy loving God that they didn't have time to love their neighbor. And that is when our routines become counterproductive. Let's be honest. We can get so busy doing "ministry" that we don't have time for ministry.

Let me put it in bumper-sticker terms: ministry happens. If you're chasing the Wild Goose, you don't have to manufacture opportunities to minister. In fact, as I read the gospels, it seems to me that *most* of Jesus' ministry was unplanned. Like the time when Jesus was walking out of Jericho and a blind man named Bartimaeus called out to him.

> When he heard that it was Jesus of Nazareth, he began to shout, "Jesus, Son of David, have mercy on me!"
> Many rebuked him and told him to be quiet, but he shouted all the more.[37]

The people who rebuked Bartimaeus saw him as a human interruption. And there is no question that Jesus had places to go and things to do. But Jesus didn't see a human interruption; He saw a divine appointment. And what did He do? "Jesus stopped."[38] Those two words speak volumes.

Spontaneity is an underappreciated dimension of spirituality. In fact, spiritual maturity has less to do with long-range visions than it does with moment-by-moment sensitivity to the promptings of the Holy Spirit. And it is our moment-by-moment sensitivity to the Holy Spirit that turns life into an everyday adventure.

HEURISTIC BIAS

Spiritual growth is a conundrum. The key to spiritual growth is developing healthy and holy routines. We call them *spiritual disciplines*. But once the routine becomes routine, we need to disrupt it. Why? Because sacred routines become empty rituals when we do them out of left-brain memory instead of right-brain imagination.

I'm certainly not suggesting that routines are bad. Most of us practice a morning ritual that includes showering, brushing our teeth, and putting on deodorant. On behalf of your family and friends, I want to encourage you to continue those routines.

But here's the Catch-22: *good routines become bad routines if we don't change the routine*. One of the greatest dangers we face spiritually is learning *how* and forgetting *why*. Call it familiarization. Call it habituation. Call it routinization. Call it what you want. When we learn how and forget why, we start going through the motions spiritually.

We tend to think and act in patterned ways. And that tendency to think the way we've always thought or do it the way we've always done it is called *heuristic bias*. It is an incredibly complex cognitive process, but the end result is mindlessness. We do things without thinking about them. And if we aren't careful, we pray without thinking, take Communion without thinking, and worship without thinking.

I read a fascinating study a few years ago that suggested people stop thinking about the lyrics of a song after singing it thirty times. I'm sure the numbers vary from person to person, but the tendency is universal. And it has profound implications when it comes to worship.

"These people say they are mine," God complained. "They honor me with their lips, but their hearts are far from me. And their worship of me is nothing but man-made rules learned by rote."[39] God doesn't want to be lip-synced. He wants to be worshiped.

When we worship out of memory, it must sound to God like a broken record. Maybe that's why the psalms exhort us no fewer than six times to sing a new song. We need new words, new postures, new thoughts, and new feelings.

Why? Because God wants to be more than a memory!

Left-brain worship doesn't cut it. Neither does left-brain prayer. Jesus warned, "When you pray, don't babble on and on as people of other religions do. They think their prayers are answered merely be repeating their words again and again. Don't be like them, for your Father knows exactly what you need even before you ask him!"[40]

It is easy to get into a prayer rut, isn't it? We repeat all the prayer clichés we know, followed by an empty "amen!"

Sometimes we pray as if God has no personality. The staff at our church knows that one dimension of my prayer life is humor. We bust out laughing in the middle of prayer all the time because I'll bust out a joke. I know that might sound sacrilegious, but I love telling jokes; why would I exclude God? And I can't imagine a relationship with someone where humor wasn't part of our conversational relationship. It would be downright boring. I'm not sure God laughs at all my jokes, but He's the one who created us with a sense of humor.

We need to quit praying out of memory and start praying out of imagination. Don't get me wrong. I certainly have some left-brain prayer mantras that I repeat all the time. One of them is a presermon prayer: "Help me help people." I pray it all the time, and I think I mean it every time. And I pray Luke 2:52 for my kids regularly. I pray that they would grow "in wisdom and stature, and in favor with God and men." Nothing wrong with those memorized prayers, but we also need to inject a little imagination.

I talked about prayer heuristics at National Community Church not long ago and challenged our congregation to pray in a different way or different place or different tone. A few days later I got an e-mail from an NCCer who did a prayer experiment:

> After your sermon at Union Station, I decided to approach
> your challenge to thank God for the daily miracles we gener-
> ally expect from Him or even forget about. Instead of waiting
> for the evening, I decided to start right then on my walk back
> to the Metro. Knowing the list of thanks could be infinitely
> long, I decided to focus my prayer of thanksgiving only on
> miracles I was receiving at the moment of my prayer.
>
> "Thank You, God, for aerobic respiration. Thank You for

mitochondria, which right now are creating ATP. Thank You for ATP. Thank You for glycolysis. Thank You for pyruvate."

With a biology degree, I ended up having a lot of things on the list. By the time I got back to my place in Arlington, I was thanking God for each of the amino acids.

"Thank You, God, for glycine. Thank you for leucine. And isoleucine. And tryptophan."

By the time I was thanking God for the fact that all organisms that form amino acids have the same chirality so that my body can reuse the nutrients and cellular building blocks of the food I break down, I found myself in absolute awe of His creation.

I prayed while I took a walk outside, thanking Him for bones and ligaments and tendons. I also thanked Him that I somehow never took an anatomy course in college, because otherwise I would have felt compelled to thank Him for each bone by name, which would have definitely set me back even more in my quest to get through most of the miracles I was receiving at that moment.

I spent the day praying without ceasing! I literally didn't stop and just consciously kept listing things I was thankful for. I listened to music and thanked Him for my ears' cochleae. While I made dinner, I thanked Him for xylem in the plants I was preparing. I spent a lot of time thanking Him for the molecular properties of water.

I thanked Him for the bacteria in my colon that help me digest food. I thanked Him for genetic recombination, which made developing and cultivating cotton plants possible for the jeans I was wearing.

By the time the sun set and it was dark at nine o'clock, I think God was amused with the futility of me trying to thank Him for everything.

The Spirit finally hushed me, saying, "You can stop now."

Now that's a right-brain prayer!

THE LAW OF REQUISITE VARIETY

According to the law of requisite variety, the survival of any system depends on its capacity to cultivate variety in its internal structures. Disequilibrium is life. Equilibrium is death. Prolonged equilibrium dulls our senses, numbs our minds, and atrophies our muscles.

In physical exercise, routines eventually become counterproductive. If you exercise the same way every time you work out, your muscles start adapting and stop growing. So you need to change the routine. You need to disorient them. The same is true spiritually.

This is precisely why we need the Wild Goose in our lives. Without Him, life becomes an empty routine or dull ritual. The Wild Goose keeps things crazy.

When I'm in a spiritual slump, nine times out of ten, something sacred has become routine. I'm sure it differs by personality, but one of the ways I snap out of a spiritual slump is by disturbing my routine and experimenting with spiritual disciplines.

Sometimes all it takes is a small change in routine. Volunteer at a local homeless shelter. Start keeping a gratitude journal. Get plugged into a small group or Bible study. Take a day off and do a personal retreat. Or just get up a little earlier in the morning and spend a little extra time with God.

One of the small changes in routine that has helped me rejuvenate my devotional times is picking up a new translation of Scripture. New words help me think new thoughts. If you typically read the Message, try out the King James. Or if you read the King James, try out the New Living Translation.

Small changes in routine can result in radical change. But sometimes getting out of a spiritual slump takes a more sustained effort. I'm an optimist by nature. I don't get down very often, and when I do, it doesn't last long. But a few years ago I hit bottom emotionally, and I didn't bounce. And the only thing that got me out of that season of discouragement was a forty-day fast. You can fast by giving up whatever you want, but I chose to give up television for forty days. And the Lord impressed on me that His hearing my voice wasn't nearly as important as my hearing His voice. So although I devoted myself to prayer, the primary focus of the fast was reading through the entire Bible during those forty days. I wasn't sure I could do it, but it's amazing how much time you have to read when you turn off the TV.

The things the Lord revealed during that forty-day fast changed my life. And I have a journal full of reflections. But one particular prayer walk on one particular day became a burning bush. I was praying near the Senate fountain that stands between Union Station and the Capitol Building, and God reminded me of a simple truth: "It's not about what you can do for Me; it's about what I have done for you." I know that doesn't sound like a revolutionary thought. But

when the truth of that statement sank into my heart, it revolutionized my life. I'll never be the same. And that Senate fountain is one
of my burning bushes.

THROW DOWN YOUR STAFF

Every summer I take a six-week preaching sabbatical. The reason is
simple. It is so easy to get focused on what God wants to do *through*
me that I totally neglect what God wants to do *in* me. So I take off
my sandals for six weeks. I go on vacation. I go to church with my
family. And for several weeks during the summer, I just sit with our
congregation, taking notes and singing songs like everyone else. My
sabbatical is one way I keep the routine from becoming routine. But
it's about more than just taking off my sandals. Let me explain.

Shortly after telling Moses to take off his sandals, God gave
Moses one more curious command. He told Moses to throw down
his staff.

> Then the LORD said to him, "What is that in your hand?"
>
> "A staff," he replied.
>
> The LORD said, "Throw it on the ground."
>
> Moses threw it on the ground and it became a snake, and
> he ran from it. Then the LORD said to him, "Reach out your
> hand and take it by the tail." So Moses reached out and took
> hold of the snake and it turned back into a staff in his hand.
> "This," said the LORD, "is so that they may believe that the
> LORD, the God of their fathers—the God of Abraham, the
> God of Isaac and the God of Jacob—has appeared to you."[41]

A shepherd's staff was a six-foot-long wooden rod that was curved at one end. It functioned as a walking stick, a weapon, and a prod used to guide the flock. Moses never left home without his staff. That staff symbolized his security. It offered him physical security from wild animals. It provided his financial security—his sheep were his financial portfolio. And it was a form of relational security. After all, Moses worked for his father-in-law.

But the staff was more than just a form of security. It was also part of his identity. When Moses looked in the mirror, he saw a shepherd—nothing more, nothing less. And I think that's why Moses asked God to send someone else. "Who am I, that I should go to Pharaoh and bring the Israelites out of Egypt?"[42] I love the way God answers his question by changing the focus. God says: "I will be with you."[43] That doesn't really seem like an answer to Moses' question, does it? But I think it was God's way of saying, *"Who* you are isn't the issue; the issue is *whose* you are!"

Has God ever called you to throw something down? Something in which you find your security or put your identity? It's awfully hard to let go, isn't it? It feels like you are jeopardizing your future. And it feels like you could lose what is most important to you. But that is when you discover who you really are.

I am surrounded by an amazing team at National Community Church. And trust me, they didn't accept job offers from NCC because of the signing bonus! They came because they felt called. One of our longest-tenured staff members is Heather Zempel, who serves as our discipleship pastor. Heather was working on Capitol Hill in a Senate office. As an environmental engineering major, she had landed her dream job working on environmental issues. Heather loved her job. And she made good money by Hill standards. Then I messed it all up. I asked her to take a position at National Community Church working longer hours while making less money. Heather could have held on to her Senate staff position. And the routine of life would have continued. But she had the courage to throw down her staff and take up a new mantle of leadership. Heather is one of the best communicators and leaders I've ever had the pleasure of working with. And NCC wouldn't be where we are or who we are without her. But it all traces back to her courage to throw down the staff, come out of the cage, and chase the Wild Goose.

I agonized with Heather when she made the decision. And I agonize with you because I know how tough it is to throw down a staff. It was so hard to throw down my scholarship at the University of Chicago. It was so hard to leave the security of friends and family and move from Chicago to Washington DC. But the only way you discover a new identity is by letting an old one go. And the only way you'll find your security in Christ is by throwing down the human securities we tend to cling to.

There is a branch of history called *counterfactual theory* that asks the what-if questions. So here's my counterfactual question: What if Moses had held on to his staff? I think the answer is simple: The shepherd's staff would have remained a shepherd's staff. I don't think God would have used Moses to deliver Israel. I think Moses would have gone right back to shepherding his flock.

If you aren't willing to throw down your staff, you forfeit the miracle that is at your fingertips. You have to be willing to let go of an old identity in order to take on a new identity. And that is what happens to Moses. This is a miracle of transformation. Not just the staff turning into a snake, but a shepherd of sheep turning into the leader of a nation. But Moses *had* to throw down the shepherd's staff in order for it to be transformed into the rod of God.

As far as we know, this is the first miracle Moses ever experienced. If Moses had held on to the staff, he would have forfeited all of those miracles. He would have spent the rest of his life counting sheep.

Where do you find your identity? What is the source of your security? Is it a title? a paycheck? a relationship? a degree? a name? There is nothing wrong with any of those things as long as you can throw them down.

If you find your security outside of Christ, you have a false sense of security. And you have a false sense of identity. As long as you hold on to your staff, you'll never know what you could have accomplished with God's help. And let me remind you of this: Your success isn't contingent upon what's in your hand. Your success is contingent upon whether God extends His mighty hand on your behalf.

So let me issue a challenge. Throw down your staff, come out of the cage, and discover the adventure on the far side of routine.

YOUR CHASE

- ⊛ How have you been stuck in a rut lately? How has it affected you spiritually?
- ⊛ What opportunities do you have in the next six months to go on a trip that could change not only your latitude but also your attitude? (Think spiritual retreat, mission trip, even vacation.)

* Busy? Maybe *super* busy? How can you open up pockets of rest and quiet in your schedule so that you can hear the call of the Wild Goose?

* How have your spiritual practices, such as worship and prayer, become predictable to the point of not making much of a difference anymore? What can you do to get back the freshness of relating to an untamed God?

* What is the "staff" that you need to "throw down"? Can you do it?

CHAPTER 4

EİGHT-FOOT CEİLİNGS

Coming Out of the Cage of Assumptions

If I were to wish for anything I should not wish for wealth and power, but for the passionate sense of what can be, for the eye which, ever young and ardent, sees the possible. Pleasure disappoints, possibility never. And what wine is so sparkling, what so fragrant, what so intoxicating as possibility.

—SØREN KIERKEGAARD

Recently I came across a rather interesting scientific study with a rather interesting title: "Is There a Paleolimnological Explanation for 'Walking on Water' in the Sea of Galilee?" Go ahead and look up *paleolimnology* if you want to. I had to.

Doron Nof, a foremost expert in oceanography and limnology, suggests that over the past several millennia a rare combination of atmospheric conditions may have caused patches of ice to float on the Sea of Galilee. Can you guess where this is going? Nof calculated that the chances of this floating-ice phenomenon happening is less than once every thousand years, but those odds didn't keep him from questioning whether Jesus walked on water after all. Maybe He was surfing on a patch of floating ice.

Want to know what I think? I think Jesus walked on water because the Bible says Jesus walked on water.[44] But I have to admit, I'm not sure which I'd rather see. Balancing on a patch of floating ice all the way to the middle of the Sea of Galilee in the middle of the night with high waves and low visibility seems almost as miraculous as walking on water.

Doron Nof says, "Whether this happened or not is an issue for religion scholars, archeologists, anthropologists, and believers to decide on. As natural scientists, we merely point out that unique freezing processes probably happened in that region several times during the last 12,000 years."[45]

Nof is a naturalist. And as a naturalist, he does not have a cognitive category for the supernatural. So Nof did what many of us do when something doesn't fit within our preexisting cognitive categories. We explain away what we cannot explain. I have that tendency. I bet you do too.

Instead of embracing the mystery, we come up with human explanations for supernatural phenomena. Instead of living in wonderment, we try to make the Omniscient One fit within the logical limits of our left brain. And if I may be so bold, I honestly don't think that makes us smart. I think it makes us small-minded. And God isn't the one diminished. We are.

Not only does God disrupt our routines, like we explored in the last chapter; He also challenges our assumptions. Assumptions that take all the mystery and majesty out of life.

CUT-AND-PASTE CHRISTIANITY

In the beginning, God made man in His image.[46] Man has been making God in his image ever since.

Call it naturalism. Call it anthropomorphism. Call it idolatry. Call it what you will. The result of this spiritual inversion is a god who is about our size and looks an awful lot like us. And most of our spiritual shortcomings stem from this fundamental mistake: thinking about God in human terms. We make God in our image, and as A. W. Tozer said in *The Knowledge of the Holy*, we're left with a god who "can never surprise us, never overwhelm us, nor astonish us, nor transcend us."[47]

Thomas Jefferson loved the teachings of Jesus. In fact, the author of the Declaration of Independence called them "the most sublime and benevolent code of morals which has ever been offered to man." But Jefferson was also a child of the Enlightenment. He didn't have a cognitive category for miracles, so Jefferson literally took a pair of scissors and cut them out of his King James Bible. It took him two or three nights. And by the time he was done, he had cut out the virgin birth, cut out the angels, cut out the Resurrection. Jefferson extracted every miracle, and the result was a book titled *The Life and Morals of Jesus of Nazareth*, or what is commonly referred to as the Jefferson Bible.

Hard to imagine, isn't it? And something rises up within those of us who believe that the Bible is inspired by God. Part of us scoffs or scolds Jefferson, *You can't pick and choose. You can't cut and paste. You can't do that to the Bible.* But here's the truth: while most of us can't imagine taking a pair of scissors to the Bible and physically cutting verses out, we do exactly what Jefferson did. We ignore verses we cannot comprehend. We avoid verses we do not like. And we rationalize verses that are too radical.

Can I make a personal confession? Whenever I'm reading the Bible and I come to a verse that I don't fully understand or live up to, I find myself reading really fast. I speed-read right past those verses. But then I slow it down when I come across verses I understand and obey. That's human nature, isn't it? Here's a lesson I've learned the hard way: when I come across a verse I want to read real fast, I probably need to read real slow!

So while we may not cut sections of the Bible out with a pair of scissors, the end result is the same. We pick and choose the truths we want to accept. We become trapped by our own logic. Our lives are limited to those things we can comprehend with our cerebral cortex. We end up in the cage of our own assumptions. And the more assumptions we make, the smaller our cage becomes.

Enter Abraham.

STARGAZING

"[God] took [Abraham] outside and said, 'Look up at the heavens and count the stars—if indeed you can count them.' Then he said to him, 'So shall your offspring be.' "[48]

It is easy to read right past this story and think nothing of it. God promised Abraham that his descendents would be as numerous as the stars in the sky. So what? But what God *did* is just as significant as what God *said*. Did you catch it? "[God] took [Abraham] outside."

Abraham was holed up inside his tent. He was staring at an eight-foot ceiling, so to speak. So God took him on a field trip and gave him an assignment: count the stars. I wonder how long it took. Maybe it was an all-nighter. But about the time Abraham lost count, God had given him an object lesson he would never forget. Abraham would never look into the sky the same way. The stars became nightly reminders of the promise God had given him.

Not long ago I went camping with my two sons, and at the end of the day we spent about fifteen minutes lying on our backs in an open field just looking at the stars. Parker pointed out some of the constellations. And Josiah pointed out the moving stars, also known as airplanes. As we looked into the expanse of space that stretches billions of light-years in every direction, it was a reminder of just how big God is. There is something about looking up into the night sky that restores my perspective and recalibrates my spirit. It reminds me of how small I am and how big God is.

When Teddy Roosevelt was president, he and his naturalist friend William Beebe would routinely go outside after dinner and look up at the night sky. They would locate a faint spot of light in the lower left-hand corner of Pegasus and recite the following:

This is the Spiral Galaxy in Andromeda.

It is as large as our Milky Way.

It is one of 100 million galaxies.

It is 750,000 light-years away.

It consists of 100 billion suns, each larger than our sun.

Roosevelt would pause and grin. Then he would say to his friend, "Now I think we feel small enough! Let's go to bed."[49]

Why did God take Abraham outside? The answer is more obvious than we imagine. As long as Abraham was inside the tent, a man-made ceiling obscured his vision. It kept the promises of God out of sight.

We have the same problem. It's like young children who have not yet developed the psychological capacity known as *object permanence*: out of sight, out of mind. We lose perspective when we lose sight of the promises of God.

God wanted to remind Abraham of just how big He was, so He told him to do a little stargazing. I think it was God's way of saying, "Don't put an eight-foot ceiling on what I can do."

SPOOKY ACTION AT A DISTANCE

In 1964, John Stewart Bell published a paper titled "On the Einstein-Podolsky-Rosen Paradox" that revolutionized quantum physics. Bell essentially disproved the principle of local causes, which states that the relationships among particles must be mediated by local forces. Bell's research indicated that, regardless of distance, everything in the universe is interconnected.

Almost all of classical physics rested upon the assumption that nothing in the universe could travel faster than the speed of light. In other words, 186,000 miles per second was assumed to be the universal speed limit. But experiments have shown that if two sub-atomic particles shoot into space as the result of a subatomic reaction, they always seem to influence each other no matter how far apart they travel. What happens to one particle happens to the other particle superluminally, or faster than the speed of light. Invisible links among all particles defy space and time. The technical term is *instantaneous nonlocality*.

Albert Einstein referred to it as "spooky action at a distance."

"Spooky action at a distance" doubles as a decent definition for the sovereignty of God, doesn't it? God is superluminal. He is God Most High and God Most Nigh.

What I'm getting at is this: we make far too many assumptions about what is and what is not possible in the physical universe. We do the same thing spiritually. And those assumptions become eight-foot ceilings that limit our lives. One of the most dangerous assumptions we can make is assuming we know more than we really do. But Scripture challenges that assumption: "The man who thinks he knows something does not yet know as he ought to know."[50]

The smartest people in the world are not the people who know the most. The smartest people are the people who know how much they don't know. Or to put it another way, the smartest people are the people who make the fewest assumptions.

In the philosophy of science, there is a concept known as *critical realism*. It is the recognition that we don't know everything there is to know, so scientific theories are subject to change based upon new discoveries. That intellectual humility, coupled with curiosity, drives scientific discovery.

We need a degree of critical realism in theology. Pride is offended when assumptions are challenged. Humility welcomes the challenge because the desire to know God is greater than the need to be right.

And humility, coupled with curiosity, drives us to keep asking, seeking, knocking.[51]

The bottom line is this: the more faith you have, the fewer assumptions you will make. Why? Because with God all things are possible.[52]

CHALLENGING ASSUMPTIONS

According to the research of Rolf Smith, children ask 125 probing questions per day. Adults, on the other hand, ask only a half dozen probing questions each day.[53] That means that somewhere between childhood and adulthood, we lose 119 questions per day.

When my son Parker was five years old, I did a little research project of my own. I was intrigued by the sheer volume and variety of Parker's questions, so I kept track of them for one week. Here is a sampling of the questions I fielded that week:

- ❋ "Why do whales live in water?"
- ❋ "Why do planes go over cars?"
- ❋ "Why do caterpillars turn into butterflies?"
- ❋ "Why do stars come out at night?"
- ❋ "Why do houses have doors?"

My favorite question was, "Why do horses bounce?" I said, "You mean trot." Parker said, "No, I mean bounce."

As part of my experiment, I wanted Parker to know that there isn't always an easy answer to every question, so I decided to turn the tables and ask him a question. I thought long and hard to come up with a question that would stump my five-year-old. The best question I could come up with was, "Parker, why does it rain?" Without a moment's hesitation, my five-year-old lowered his voice to a let-me-tell-you-the-way-the-world-works tone and replied, "Because everything is thirsty."

Hey, I tried.

Children are born with a holy curiosity. If we had a nickel for every time they ask us *why,* we might actually be able to pay for their college education. And not only are they interested in everything, but they also believe everything is possible. Children don't make assumptions. They swim in the sea of possibilities.

Unfortunately, at some point in our lives, most of us stop asking questions and start making assumptions. We stop gazing at the stars and start staring at the ceiling. And that is when we need to get married and start a family.

Thank God for children! I think God gives us children for lots of reasons, one of which is to challenge our adult assumptions. My children don't just play make-believe. That is the effect they have on me. They make me believe.

As a father, I have a responsibility to teach my kids. But I wonder if I have an even greater responsibility to learn from them. After all, Jesus said: "Unless you change and become like little children, you will never enter the kingdom of heaven."[54]

One of our kids' favorite DC destinations is the National Air and Space Museum. It is only a few blocks from our home, so we'll occasionally spend an afternoon retracing the history of aviation from kites to rockets. On one visit, when Josiah was a toddler, a cross section of an American Airlines Douglas DC-7 airplane was on display. As we prepared to board, I noticed a look of concern on Josiah's face. I asked him if he wanted to get on the airplane, and he asked me, "It not take off?"

Lora and I couldn't help but laugh because of the implausibility. There was no engine, no wings, and no runway. It was a twenty-foot cross section of a plane! Yet Josiah thought it might take off. In fact, at every exhibit we visited that afternoon, he asked, "It not take off?"

That is the beauty of childhood. Children do not know what cannot be done. They have not yet defined what is and what is not possible. No assumptions. No impossibilities. No eight-foot ceilings. The only limitation they know is their God-given imagination.

One historical footnote since we're on the topic of flying.

In the 1870s, an annual church conference was held at Westfield College in Illinois. During the conference, the president of the college prophetically said, "We are approaching a time of great inventions. For example, I believe the day is not far off when men will fly through the air like birds."

One bishop present accused him of heresy. "The Bible tells us that flight is reserved for the angels!"[55]

The bishop's last name? Wright. His two sons, Orville and Wilbur, recorded the first successful powered flight at Kitty Hawk, North Carolina, on December 17, 1903.

Where would we be if it weren't for children who challenge our assumptions?

AGAINST ALL HOPE

Here's an assumption: ninety-year-old women don't have babies.

Fair assumption, right? It is anatomically, biologically, and gynecologically impossible for a barren, postmenopausal woman to have a child. Or is it?

Against all hope, Abraham in hope believed and so became
the father of many nations, just as it had been said to him,
"So shall your offspring be." Without weakening in his faith,
he faced the fact that his body was as good as dead—since
he was about a hundred years old—and that Sarah's womb
was also dead. Yet he did not waver through unbelief regard-
ing the promise of God, but was strengthened in his faith
and gave glory to God, being fully persuaded that God had
power to do what he had promised.[56]

Faith is not logical. But it isn't illogical either. Faith is *theo*logical.
It does not ignore reality; it just adds God into the equation. Abraham "faced the fact." But he was also "fully persuaded" that God had
the power to deliver on His promise. Faith is not mindless ignorance;
it simply refuses to limit God to the logical constraints of the left
brain.

Think of it this way. Logic questions God. Faith questions assumptions. And at the end of the day, faith is trusting God more
than you trust your own assumptions.

So let me ask you a question: what eight-foot ceilings have you
placed on God? What promises have you given up on? What assumptions are keeping you caged?

One common assumption that keeps us caged is this: *I'm too old.*
That is the assumption Abraham had to challenge. He was one hundred years old. "His body was as good as dead." But against all hope
he kept hoping.

We have a core value at NCC: it's never too late to become who
you might have been. The Bible is full of late bloomers. Jesus was

thirty years old before He transitioned from carpentry to ministry. Moses didn't assume leadership until he was an octogenarian. And Noah was in his five hundreds when he built the ark.

I don't care how old you are, if you're still breathing, it means God isn't finished with you yet.

One of my heroes is a woman named Harriet Doerr. In a day when most women never even thought about a college education, she dreamed of earning a degree. However, life circumstances got in the way. Money then marriage then kids kept her from achieving her goal. But the dream never died. Harriet earned her bachelor's degree from Stanford when she was sixty-seven years old. And she wrote her first novel, *Stones for Ibarra,* when she was seventy-three. And it didn't just get published; it won the National Book Award in 1984.

I love Harriet's outlook on aging. "One of the best things about aging is being able to watch imagination overtake memory."

If you stay in the cage of your assumptions, memory will overtake imagination. If you chase the Wild Goose, imagination will overtake memory.

READY OR NOT

You're never too old to go on a Wild Goose chase. Of course, you're never *too young* either. Our inexperience leads to another false assumption that keeps us caged. David was a kid when he fought Goliath. Most scholars believe Mary was a teenager when she gave birth to Jesus. And the disciples were probably twentysomethings. If age or experience were qualifications, none of them would have done what they did.

In my experience, God loves using us before we feel like we're ready. In fact, I'm not even sure Jesus thought He was ready to make the transition from carpentry to ministry. Remember what He said at the wedding of Cana before performing His first miracle? "My time has not yet come."[57] There's a hint of hesitation, isn't there? I find that fascinating and encouraging.

I realize Jesus' statement has deeper meaning. And Jesus was waiting to reveal His power until the Holy Spirit released Him into ministry. But that doesn't negate the fact that Jesus felt like He wasn't prepared yet. And I can relate to that feeling of unreadiness. It took a little prompting from His mother to get Jesus to overcome His human hesitation and step into His divine calling.

I wasn't ready to get married. Lora and I weren't ready to have kids. After all, we *were* kids. And I certainly wasn't ready to pastor National Community Church. Sure, I had taken lots of classes. But the only experience on my résumé was one summer internship, and all I did was organize the men's softball league!

What I'm getting at is this: you'll never be ready.

PERSONAL ASSUMPTIONS

As I look back on my own Wild Goose chase, the defining moments of my life are the moments when my assumptions were challenged and I had a choice to make: hang on to my assumptions or hang on to God. You cannot do both!

Assumption: It doesn't make sense to give up a full-ride scholarship to a top-ranked university.

The University of Chicago paid my way to go to school. By the end of my freshman year, I had a starting position on the basketball team. And the U of C was the third-ranked school in the country academically that year. On paper, it was a perfect setup. It made no sense to give up that scholarship. And it definitely took some pulling and prodding and prompting by the Wild Goose. But I finally let go of my academic and occupational assumptions, transferred to Central Bible College, and started preparing for my life calling.

I wouldn't trade my time at the University of Chicago for anything. But if I hadn't challenged that assumption, I never would have been prepared to go into a church plant at twenty-six. If I had stayed at the University of Chicago, it would have become a cage for me.

Assumption: Movie theaters are short-term rental options.

I went into church planting with the traditional mind-set: meet in rented facilities until you can buy or build a church building. Then we started meeting in the movie theaters at Union Station. We have comfortable seats, huge screens, and the smell of popcorn every weekend. Why build a church building? Besides that, property on Capitol Hill goes for about $10 million an acre. At some point we stopped viewing theaters as short-term rental options, and they became our long-term multisite strategy.

Our vision of meeting in movie theaters at Metro stops throughout the DC area challenges the assumption that you need a church building to grow a church. And that assumption is being challenged all across the country. Hundreds of churches are now meeting at a theater near you. And I dream of the day when a church is meeting in every movie theater in America.

Don't stay in the cage just because *it's never been done that way before.*

Assumption: Churches don't build coffeehouses.

Building a coffeehouse before you build a church building seems counterintuitive. So why did we do it? Because Jesus didn't just hang out in synagogues. He also hung out at wells. Wells weren't just a place to draw water; they were natural gathering places in ancient culture. Coffeehouses are postmodern wells.

Doing church in marketplace environments is part of our DNA at NCC. And building a coffeehouse was a way of creating a "third place," to use the sociological term coined by Ray Oldenburg. We wanted to create a place, besides work and home, where the church and community could cross paths. Every day we serve hundreds of customers. And we don't just serve coffee; we serve Christ. Many of our customers end up connecting with Christ at one of our coffeehouse services.

I'm not sure what assumptions you need to challenge. They can be difficult to identify. But for most of us, our inexperience, inability, or lack of knowledge keeps us in the cage. We feel unqualified because of something we have not done, cannot do, or do not know.

If it's any encouragement, not one person on our staff had ever worked at a coffeehouse when we started out on that Wild Goose chase. Don't get me wrong. We did our homework. We came up with a business plan. And our business-manager-turned-coffeehouse-manager, Christina Borja, went to work at Starbucks for six months to learn the business. But we were absolutely inexperienced and un-knowledgeable when we purchased the property and started build-ing our coffeehouse. We had no business going into the coffeehouse business. But we didn't assume that our inexperience, inability, or lack of knowledge should keep us from doing what we knew the Holy Spirit was calling us to do.

If you want more adventure in your life, come out of the cage of your assumptions. Don't assume that you cannot start the business or write the book or overcome the addiction or get the job or save the marriage. Quit assuming and start believing.

"I AM ABLE"

It seems to me that the people God uses the most are those who make the fewest assumptions. Joshua didn't assume that the sun could not stand still. Elisha didn't assume that an iron ax head can-not float. Mary didn't assume that virgins cannot get pregnant. Peter didn't assume that he could not walk on water. And Jesus didn't assume that dead people cannot be raised to life again.

When we put our faith in Christ, we allow the One who changed the molecular structure of water and turned it into wine to redefine what is and is not possible. And that changes everything because "I can do everything through [Christ] who gives me strength."[58]

When I was in the eighth grade, a visitation team from our church came to our house to pray and asked if they could "agree in prayer" with us about anything. I'd had asthma since I was three years old and had been hospitalized half a dozen times with pulmonary complications. So we held hands and prayed that God would heal my asthma.

Well, I still have asthma. But as a result of the team coming to visit, something remarkable did happen that I will never forget. When I woke up the next morning, all the warts on my feet were gone! I kid you not. My first thought was that there must have been some kind of prayer mix-up. *Did God answer the wrong prayer? Maybe someone else somewhere else is breathing great but still has warts on his feet.* It seemed like there was some confusion between here and heaven. I didn't get what I ordered.

And that is when I heard what I would describe as the inaudible yet unmistakable voice of God: *I just wanted you to know that I am able.*

I don't experience miracles like this right and left. I'm guessing that my prayer batting average is no better than yours. And I don't hear the voice of God as often or as clearly as I would like. But it is difficult to doubt after an experience like this. God doesn't always answer my prayers how or when I want Him to. But I do live my life with this fundamental conviction: God is able.

THE BEST I CAN DO

For the past several months, I've had a recurring thought: *I don't want to live my life in such a way that the best I can do is the best I can do.* Frankly, my best isn't good enough.

When I fail to pray, the best I can do is the best I can do. I forfeit my spiritual potential. But when I pray, the best I can do is no longer the best I can do. The best I can do is the best *God* can do. And He is able to do immeasurably more than all I can ask or imagine.[59] Prayer is one way we overcome our assumptions and escape our space-time limitations.

When I fail to give, the best I can do is the best I can do. I am keeping God out of the equation of my finances. But when I tithe, I am standing on the promises of God.[60] And in my experience, God can do more with 90 percent than I can do with 100 percent. In addition, tithing is not just good stewardship; it turns money management into a financial adventure.

When Lora and I got married, we made a decision that we would never not tithe. We give the first 10 percent of everything we make back to God because we believe it belongs to Him. But honestly, the real adventure began when we started giving above and beyond the tithe.

Right after moving to DC, I pioneered a parachurch ministry, and we had to raise our own budget by traveling to churches and asking for money. We lived offering to offering until we started giving beyond our ability. About the time we reached 50 percent of budget, I felt prompted by God to give a financial gift to another parachurch ministry in the city.

On a human level, it didn't make sense. How can you give what you don't have? I easily could have justified waiting until we had raised our full budget, but I knew that if I didn't obey the prompting, I would never see where the Wild Goose chase would take us. I still remember the mixed emotions I felt as I wrote that $350 check.

It was painful and joyful. It was a difficult check to write, but I knew in my spirit that God was going to honor our financial faith. I sealed the envelope, walked to the post office near my office, and dropped it in the mailbox outside. Then I walked inside to retrieve my mail. Inside my post office box was a check for ten thousand dollars.

Sometimes we fail to connect the dots between our faith and God's faithfulness, but when sixty seconds is all that separates your giving from God's blessing, it's tough to miss the point. And the point is, when you give beyond your ability, God will bless you beyond your ability. Don't get me wrong. God is not a slot machine. If you give for the wrong reasons, God won't honor it. But if your motives are right, the law of measures kicks in: "With the measure you use, it will be measured to you."[61]

You cannot outgive God. And you not only get back; you get back *more* than you gave up. The best you can do is no longer the best you can do; the best you can do is the best *God* can do. And God can miraculously provide a 2757 percent ROI in sixty seconds.

For the record, Abraham was the first person in the Bible known to have tithed.[62] He managed money the way he managed the rest of his life: by faith.

Don't allow financial greed or fear to keep you in the cage. Living generously is way too fun and way too exciting. Too many of us allow a scarcity mentality to keep us in the cage. We assume that the more we give, the less we'll have. That is an unbiblical assumption.

Tithing is trusting. And when you put God first financially, you live with sanctified expectations. You can't wait to see the wild ways in which the Wild Goose is going to provide.

THE LAST LAUGH

I wish I could tell you that God always delivers on His promises in sixty seconds flat. Sometimes He does, but more often He doesn't.

God called Abraham out of Ur when he was 75, but Isaac wasn't born until Abraham turned 100. God delivered on His promise, but it took 25 years. That is 300 months, 1,300 weeks, or 9,125 days!

> Now the LORD was gracious to Sarah as he had said, and the LORD did for Sarah what he had promised. Sarah became pregnant and bore a son to Abraham in his old age, at the very time God had promised him. Abraham gave the name Isaac to the son Sarah bore him. When his son Isaac was eight days old, Abraham circumcised him, as God commanded him. Abraham was a hundred years old when his son Isaac was born to him.
>
> Sarah said, "God has brought me laughter, and everyone who hears about this will laugh with me." And she added, "Who would have said to Abraham that Sarah would nurse children? Yet I have borne him a son in his old age."[63]

Waiting twenty-five years for God to fulfill His promise must have seemed like an eternity to Abraham and Sarah. It had to be spiritually confusing and emotionally exhausting. In that culture, barrenness was considered a curse. And Sarah not only lived with that social stigma, but I'm guessing she also felt a twinge of sadness every time she was around children. The sound of children's laughter caused tears because it was a reminder of what she wanted but could not have.

I wonder if, as the years passed, Abraham and Sarah lost some of the laughter. It is hard to laugh when you feel a deep sadness that never goes away. And that is why Isaac's name is so apropos. Isaac means "laughter." To be honest, I used to think the name was a punishment because Sarah laughed at God when God said she would have a baby,[64] but I have changed my mind based on circumstantial evidence.

A child's laugh is priceless. Nothing brings me greater joy than hearing my kids laugh. God is no different. God loves it when we laugh. And Isaac was God's way of giving Abraham and Sarah their laughter back. He is the God who conceives laughter.

I also think Isaac's name reveals a dimension of God's character. When Sarah laughed at God, He said, "Is anything too hard for the LORD?"[65] Part of me wonders if God waited twenty-five years, until the thought of Sarah having a baby was absolutely inconceivable (pun intended). And then He broke through the eight-foot ceiling and proved once again that nothing is too hard for Him. Isaac was God's way of saying, "I'm going to have the last laugh."

TERRA INCOGNITA

God didn't just bless Abraham with a son. Abraham became the father of a nation. And that nation gave birth to the Savior of the world. But like every Wild Goose chase, it all started with one small step of faith. "By faith Abraham, when called to go to a place he would later receive as his inheritance, obeyed and went, even though he did not know where he was going."[66]

Abraham is the patron saint of Wild Goose chases. He had no idea where he was going, but he did not let that keep him in the cage. By faith he ventured into the unknown. He left behind his family, his home, and his assumptions.

Outside Union Station in Washington DC, there is a large statue honoring Christopher Columbus. The plaque beneath the statue says: "To the memory of Christopher Columbus whose high faith and indomitable courage gave to mankind a new world."

On the edge of medieval maps, cartographers used to inscribe the Latin phrase *terra incognita*. Naysayers and doomsdayers believed that if you ventured too far into unknown territory, you would either fall off the edge of the flat earth or run into two-headed dragons. But that didn't keep a few brave souls from venturing into uncharted waters.

Columbus was actually trying to find a westward route to the Indies, something many experts assumed was impossible. But Columbus challenged the assumption and embarked on a Wild Goose chase. Columbus was no saint. In his own diary, he confessed: "I am a most unworthy sinner." But Columbus also stated that it wasn't intelligence, mathematics, or maps that made his voyage a success. Columbus credited the Holy Spirit with the idea. "It was the Lord who put it into my mind, (I could feel His hand upon me), the fact that it would be possible to sail from here to the Indies. All who heard of my project rejected it with laughter, ridiculing me. There is no question that the inspiration was from the Holy Spirit, because He comforted me with rays of marvelous inspiration from the Holy Scriptures."[67]

Here is what impresses me the most about Columbus's voyage: not one crew member had ever been more than three hundred miles offshore!

In the words of André Gide, "People cannot discover new lands until they have the courage to lose sight of the shore."

The Wild Goose is always calling us into terra incognita. That is where adventure is found. But you have to come out of the cage of your assumptions. You have to be willing to go somewhere you've never been or do something you've never done. And if you have the faith to take the first step, God will have the last laugh.

YOUR CHASE

- ⊛ In the past, when have you made a false assumption about God or His will for your life? How did you discover your error?
- ⊛ What assumptions do you think could be limiting God in your life right now? How can you challenge those assumptions?
- ⊛ What risks are you running if you cling to your assumptions?
- ⊛ What would it mean for imagination to overtake memory in your life?
- ⊛ Is there any area of your life where you feel like you have lost your laughter? Why? And how do you think you can get it back?

CHAPTER 5

A ROOSTER'S CROW

Coming Out of the Cage of Guilt

Your worst days are never so bad that you are
beyond the reach of His grace. And your best
days are never so good that you are beyond the
need of God's grace. Every day should be a day
of relating to God on the basis of His grace
alone.

—JERRY BRIDGES

Around the turn of the twentieth century, a Russian psycholo-
gist and physician named Ivan Pavlov performed some
groundbreaking experiments that won him a Nobel Prize. Dogs naturally salivate for food, but Pavlov wanted to see if salivation could
be caused by another stimulus. As you may remember from a high
school science class, Pavlov conditioned the dogs by ringing a bell
before feeding them. Eventually ringing the bell, without the food,

was enough in itself to cause salivation. Pavlov referred to this learned relationship as a *conditioned reflex*.

To one degree or another, all of us are Pavlovian. We have been consciously and subconsciously conditioned our entire lives. And much of our behavior is dictated by those conditioned reflexes.

Every time I fill up my gas tank, I instinctively look in the side-view mirror before driving off. Why? Because a few years ago I ripped a gas hose right out of a gas pump. I was wondering why everyone was staring at us as we pulled out of the gas station. Then we heard a strange noise behind us that got louder as we drove faster. It was the sound of the gas hose dragging behind the car. Let's just say that confessing this to the teenage attendant ranks right up there on my list of most embarrassing moments. And even though I've filled up our gas tank countless times since then without incident, I always have a subconscious feeling that I've forgotten to remove the hose from the car. For me, double-checking the side-view mirror is a conditioned reflex.

Over the course of our lifetime, we acquire an elaborate repertoire of conditioned reflexes. Some of them are minor idiosyncrasies, such as a nervous laugh or half smile. Others become major personality traits. A critical personality is often born out of psychological insecurity. We criticize in others what we don't like about ourselves. Some conditioned reflexes are as natural and normal as a blush. Others are as destructive as drinking to drown your sorrows. But whether they are big or small, conscious or subconscious, harmless or harmful, one thing is certain: we are far more conditioned than we realize. And part of spiritual growth is recognizing how we have been conditioned and allowing God to recondition the reflexes that need to change.

When we sin, guilt is a healthy and holy reflex. Thank God for the conviction of the Holy Spirit that drives us to repentance. But some conditioned reflexes are like psychological straitjackets that immobilize us emotionally, relationally, and spiritually. False guilt is a great example.

The moment we confess our sin to God, our sin is forgiven and forgotten.[68] But for most of us, it is far easier to accept God's forgiveness than it is to forgive ourselves. Why? Because we can forgive, but unlike God, we cannot forget. If we don't allow the grace of God to saturate and sanctify our sinful memories, we continue to experience false guilt over confessed sin. We become so fixated on past mistakes that we forfeit future opportunities. We mistakenly think our mistakes disqualify us from being used by God. And our feelings of guilt become the cage that keeps us from chasing the Wild Goose.

Whether you are experiencing true guilt that is a by-product of *unconfessed* sin or false guilt that is the by-product of *confessed* sin, both forms of guilt dull your spiritual sense of adventure. And you won't be able to chase the Wild Goose until you get past your guilty feelings. The good news is that there is forgiveness and freedom because of what Christ accomplished on the cross. And if you receive His grace, it will not only recondition your spiritual reflexes; it will transform your life.

Enter Peter.

A TWINGE OF GUILT

Looking at Scripture through the filter of Ivan Pavlov is an interesting exercise. And Peter in particular makes a fascinating case study.

Seizing him, they led [Jesus] away and took him into the
house of the high priest. Peter followed at a distance. But
when they had kindled a fire in the middle of the courtyard
and had sat down together, Peter sat down with them. A
servant girl saw him seated there in the firelight. She looked
closely at him and said, "This man was with him."

But he denied it. "Woman, I don't know him," he said.

A little later someone else saw him and said, "You also
are one of them."

"Man, I am not!" Peter replied.

About an hour later another asserted, "Certainly this fellow was with him, for he is a Galilean."

Peter replied, "Man, I don't know what you're talking
about!" Just as he was speaking, the rooster crowed. The Lord
turned and looked straight at Peter. Then Peter remembered
the word the Lord had spoken to him: "Before the rooster
crows today, you will disown me three times." And he went
outside and wept bitterly.[69]

I've read the story of Peter's denial countless times over the years,
but I had a Pavlovian thought not long ago: *I wonder if Peter felt a
twinge of guilt every time he heard a rooster crow?*

Have you noticed the way different stimuli trigger different
memories? Seemingly insignificant sights, sounds, and smells can
evoke powerful memories. Whenever I hear "You Got It" playing on
the radio (which isn't often anymore), I have a flashback to one of
my first dates with Lora. We were driving northbound on Lakeshore
Drive from the University of Chicago toward downtown Chicago

when we heard the song for the first time. Or one whiff of lilacs, and I'm transported across time and space to my grandma's garden in Fridley, Minnesota.

I wonder if a rooster's crow had the same kind of effect on Peter. He let Jesus down when Jesus needed him most. And I've got to think that sound triggered something in his auditory cortex. It had a Pavlovian effect on Peter. Every time a rooster crowed, Peter was right back in his cage of guilt.

I think this is one of those Bible stories that is difficult for urbanites and suburbanites to fully appreciate. I live in the city, so I wake up to the sounds of the city—garbage trucks, car alarms, and police sirens. I think the rooster population in DC is zero. But if you've ever traveled to a third-world country, you know that roosters still rule the roost.

I'll never forget waking up on the island of Isabella in the Galápagos. It was like waking up to a rooster choir. There were more roosters on the island than humans. Weren't they supposed to wait until the sun came up to crow? Not these roosters. No internal clocks. And no snooze buttons! I got a rude awakening right in the middle of a REM cycle.

Imagine what it must have been like for Peter to wake up to a rooster's crow every morning. What a way to start the day! A daily reminder of his greatest failure.

Scripture says that Satan "prowls around like a roaring lion."[70] I also think he crows like a rooster. Satan is the accuser of the brothers,[71] and his tactics have not changed since the Garden of Eden. He wants to remind you of your greatest failures over and over again. Why? Because if you focus all your energy on past failures, you'll have no energy left over to dream kingdom dreams or pursue kingdom purposes. Satan wants to turn you into a reactionary. Jesus came to recondition your spiritual reflexes with His grace. And when you've been reconditioned by His grace, you will become a revolutionary for His cause.

CHIEF OF SINNERS

Several years ago, a close friend of mine found himself in prison for some crimes he had the courage to confess to. And prison life definitely took its toll. He served nearly seven years of his sentence, but I think he aged at least fourteen. Prison certainly wasn't part of his life plan. And it was a long, lonely road. But his years in prison turned into a Wild Goose chase of sorts.

While he was in prison, we exchanged letters every few months, along with occasional phone conversations. And the thing I marveled at was his refusal to feel sorry for himself. He didn't blame God for the mistakes he had made. And although his body was imprisoned, his spirit was set free because of the grace of God. My friend actually had the audacity to refer to prison as an opportunity in disguise. He earned his GED. He led chapel services. And he found countless opportunities to share his faith with other inmates.

My friend could have hardened his heart and lived the rest of his life in a cage of guilt. His mistakes could have filled him with unending regret and remorse. Yet I know very few people who have a deeper appreciation for the grace of God. And it is the grace of God that has helped my friend maintain a soft heart and an optimistic outlook on life.

My friend's story reminds me of the apostle Paul. No one has written more eloquently about the grace of God. And the reason is simple. By Paul's own admission, he was the chief of sinners.[72] I can't help but wonder if the heights of grace are attainable only after experiencing the depths of guilt.

In the words of C. S. Lewis, "When a man is getting better he understands more and more clearly the evil that is still left in him. When a man is getting worse he understands his own badness less and less." If you understand that, you're getting better. If you don't, you aren't.

I'm afraid that our therapeutic approach to faith sometimes causes us to minimize our sinfulness in a human attempt to feel better about ourselves. But all that does is short-circuit our understanding and appreciation of God's grace. We can't appreciate the full extent of God's grace until we realize the full extent of our sin. Then, and only then, can we chase the Wild Goose and His will for us with passion.

REACT LIKE A CHRISTIAN

In my experience, it is much easier to *act* like a Christian than it is to *react* like one. Most of us are good actors—we can play the part. But our reactions reveal who we really are. And maybe that is why Jesus focused so much of His teaching on reconditioning reflexes.

Pray for those who persecute you.

Love your enemies.

Bless those who curse you.

If someone forces you to go one mile, go with him two miles.

If someone strikes you on the right cheek, turn to him the other also.[73]

What is the natural reaction when someone slaps you? You feel like slapping him back, right? But the supernatural reaction is both counterintuitive and counterreactive. Jesus taught us to turn the other cheek. Think of it as spiritual aikido. We absorb the sinful energy of others and convert it into a righteous response. So persecution becomes a catalyst for prayer. Hatred inspires love. And we convert curses into blessings.[74]

Is there somebody in your life who brings out the worst in you? When you're around her, you react in ways you later regret. Or maybe it's someone who gets on your nerves or under your skin. Here's my advice: pray for them! Nothing reconditions our spiritual reflexes like prayer. Start praying for the difficult people in your life, and it will change the way you feel about them.

Have you ever wondered how Jesus was able to forgive Peter after his betrayal? We assume that Jesus was going to forgive him because He is the Son of God. But come on, His best friend had let him down at the worst possible time. If you were Jesus, wouldn't you be tempted to at least hold a little grudge and bring it up at opportune times? So how did Jesus do it? How did He forgive so freely and fully? I think the answer is surprisingly simple: Jesus prayed for Peter. "Simon, Simon, Satan has asked to sift you as wheat. But I have prayed for you, Simon, that your faith may not fail."[75]

And praying to forgive others doesn't just make you feel better about them; it keeps you on your path to spiritual adventure.

When our church purchased the piece of property where our coffeehouse on Capitol Hill now stands, there was an underlying risk. If our efforts to rezone the property from residential to commercial failed, we wouldn't be able to build. Overall, we had tremendous community backing since we were turning a crackhouse into a coffeehouse. But during the rezoning process we discovered that some influential neighbors had decided to oppose our rezoning efforts because of some misinformation about what we planned to do. I followed a link to a Web site that had posted some nasty stuff about NCC. And to be honest, I was ticked off. Their opposition had the potential to undermine our dream of building a coffeehouse, and I got angrier every time I thought about it. But somehow God gave me the grace to pray about it each time I got upset. It's about as close as I've ever come to praying without ceasing!

Thank God for the pressure valve called prayer. I don't know what I would've done if I didn't have an outlet for my anger. I started praying for the people who were opposing us, and I'll never forget the feeling I had as I walked into our zoning hearing a few months later. I had no animosity toward those who were opposing us. None whatsoever. I was able to sincerely smile and genuinely greet them because the grace of God had reconditioned my reflexes. In fact, I felt an unexplainable compassion for the people who opposed us.

The opposition eventually defused. Only three people showed up to oppose our rezoning, while more than a hundred supporters packed the committee room. And not only did we win unanimous approval, but one of the people who opposed us is now a regular customer at Ebenezers.

The ordeal was emotionally and spiritually exhausting for me. But when it was over, I thanked God for the opposition we encountered. It galvanized our resolve. It unified us as a church. And I discovered

that the Enemy's attacks become counterproductive when we coun-
teract them with prayer.

So thank God for opposition. It forces us to pray like it depends
on God, which it does. And it reconditions our reflexes in the process.

CAUGHT IN THE ACT

We have a core value at National Community Church: *love people
when they least expect it and least deserve it.* That was Jesus' modus
operandi. He went around touching lepers, eating with tax collec-
tors, hanging out with Samaritans, and befriending prostitutes.

Remember the woman caught in the act of adultery? Talk about
a moment of vulnerability. Can you say awkward? This woman was
literally caught in the act. Then the religious leaders dragged her into
the temple courts, picked up some stones, and asked Jesus a Catch-
22 question: "Teacher, this woman was caught in the act of adultery.
In the Law Moses commanded us to stone such women. Now what
do you say?"[76]

According to Levitical law, this woman deserved to die. And I'm
guessing part of her wanted to at that moment. Imagine the humili-
ation and shame. But Jesus did what Jesus does. He loved this
woman when she least expected it and least deserved it. He came to
the defense of a defenseless woman. And His answer was both bril-
liant and compassionate: "If any one of you is without sin, let him
be the first to throw a stone at her."[77]

One by one the woman's accusers dropped their stones and
walked away, from the oldest to the youngest. The only person left,
the only person who met the qualification He had established, was

Jesus Himself. Then Jesus said to the woman, "Go now and leave your life of sin."[78] And this woman walked off the pages of Scripture.

One of the reasons I anticipate heaven is because I want to hear the rest of the story. I want to know what happened to this woman. Or for that matter, what happened to the paralyzed man whose four friends lowered him through the ceiling? Or the daughter of Jairus who was raised from the dead? Or the little boy who gave Jesus five loaves and two fish? Or the man who had a legion of demons cast out of him? They walked right off the pages of Scripture. And only eternity will tell the rest of the story.

But I have a hunch that the woman caught in the act of adultery was never the same. Sure, she still had to live with the consequences of her sin and pick up the pieces of her life. But Jesus turned a moment of vulnerability into the defining moment of her life. His grace gave her a new start.

MOMENTS OF VULNERABILITY

My grandfather died when I was six years old, but not before having a profound impact on my life. He gave me my first glimpse of grace.

My grandfather had a fossil collection that was both rare and valuable, the only thing that was off-limits to me when we went over to my grandparents' house. It was the Tree of the Knowledge of Good and Evil. And you can call me Adam. One day I couldn't resist the temptation to handle one of the fossils. I'll never forget the feeling as it slipped out of my hands. That fossil wasn't the only thing that broke into pieces when it hit the floor; so did my four-year-old heart. I can still feel the intense emotions several decades later.

I knew what I had done was wrong. And I expected and deserved to be disciplined. So I was totally unprepared for my grandfather's graceful reaction. He walked into the room, assessed the situation, and picked me up to give me a hug. He didn't scold me. He didn't tell me that what I had done was wrong. All he did was hold me. It was the most graceful hug I've ever received, and without his uttering a word, I heard him say loud and clear, "Mark, you're far more valuable to me than a fossil collection."

If you want to impact someone's life, love them when they least expect it and least deserve it. When people blow it, you have an opportunity to impact their lives forever. You might think, *But they don't deserve it*. That's the point, isn't it? Do *you* deserve the grace of God?

I'm certainly not saying you don't need discernment. And there are times when discipline will bear more fruit than letting someone off the hook. But I wonder if we're afraid of loving people when they don't deserve it because it might be perceived as a tacit approval of their actions. That doesn't keep God from loving us when we least expect it and least deserve it. In fact, God is at His best when we are at our worst. "While we were still sinners, Christ died for us."[79]

Most of us are good at loving people when everything is going great. Fulfilling the "for better" part of the marriage vow, for example, is pretty easy. It's the "for worse" part that gets us every time. When Lora is at her best, I'm on my game. But when she is at her worst (hypothetically speaking, of course), it often brings out the worst in me. Why? Because we are reactive. And that is when I feel like a failure as a husband, father, and leader. I lose my temper or lose my patience. And I reactively say something or do something I later regret. In my experience, our greatest regrets are often our worst reactions. But God never reacts out of character. Amazing, isn't it? Of all our heavenly Father's qualities, I think His patience may be the most impressive.

God's love is proactive. He doesn't wait for us to get our act together. God always makes the first move. And we're called to follow suit.

A few years ago, I challenged our church to love someone who least expected it and least deserved it. I received this e-mail from an NCCer that accepted the challenge:

I am currently on an airplane headed west to meet a man
I haven't placed my eyes on in twenty years. The man is my
dad. One of your sermons began the process that brought
me to this point. It became evident to me that the single
greatest fear in my life was abandonment. This fear shaped
every aspect of how I viewed the world. There has always
been a lingering sense in my heart that I was likely to love
someone, not have my love accepted, and then be aban-
doned. My perception short-circuited every meaningful relationship I've ever had. It was through your sermon that I
realized the root of my destructive thinking and began to
do something about it.

I can recall a profound two-week period prior to my
thirtieth birthday when I struggled with the question "Have
I spent the last thirty years, the majority of the time, hating

everything and everyone?" I couldn't answer the question definitively. I could look back over my life and see the carnage left in my wake of hurt and destruction.

Your message revealed to me how to remove from my life the anchor that was keeping me from accomplishing what God has in store for me. If I was going to love anyone "who least expected it and least deserved it," that person needed to be my dad. So here I am on a plane bound to meet a man I last saw in 1983, trusting the Lord and desiring to realize the fullness of seeing His work with all of my heart.

Is there someone in your life you need to forgive? I have no idea who it is. And I have no idea how he or she hurt you. But I can unequivocally say that you need to forgive that person. Why? For starters, Jesus told us to forgive seventy times seven.[80] Do it because it is the right thing to do. But beyond that, forgiveness is the way we unplug from the past.

So many people are prisoners to one or two or three experiences in their past. A tiny seed of bitterness turns into a forest of unforgiveness. And what so many people fail to realize is that their unforgiveness doesn't hurt the person who hurt them; it simply compounds the pain in their own hearts. We think our unforgiveness will somehow cage the person who hurt us, but it only cages us. And that is where many Wild Goose chases get stalled.

Who do you need to forgive? By definition it won't be someone who deserves it. It wouldn't be grace if they deserved it. But if you have the courage to forgive them, it will set you free. And it will recondition your heart in the process.

EYE CONTACT

I'm not sure what mistakes you've made. I don't know what sinful memories are etched onto your cerebral cortex. And I have no idea what failures form the cage of guilt around your life. But I do know this: God hasn't given up on you. He can't. It's not in His nature.

There are moments in our lives when we fail so badly that we feel absolutely unworthy to receive the grace of God. And it is those moments of vulnerability that make us or break us spiritually. Either we lock ourselves in the cage of guilt and never come out, or we discover new dimensions of God's grace.

"The Lord turned and looked straight at Peter."[81] It's a footnote in the text, but I think it speaks volumes. The split second after Peter denied knowing Jesus, Jesus looked straight at him and made eye contact. I don't think it was a look of condemnation. No evil eyes. I think Jesus knew that Peter would beat himself up over this. Jesus wasn't about to give up on Peter, but He knew that Peter might give up on Peter.

Peter's denial doubled as his moment of greatest spiritual vulnerability. And that is precisely when Jesus made eye contact. Why? Because the act of making eye contact establishes a relational connection. Have you ever asked your kids to look you in the eyes when you want the truth, the whole truth, and nothing but the truth? Or silently gazed into the eyes of the one you love? Or avoided eye contact with someone you've been gossiping about? Looking someone in the eyes is an intimate act. If you look long enough, you'll see into the other's soul. And he or she will see into yours.

Jesus didn't need to say a word. In fact, if Jesus had verbalized something to Peter, it would have exposed Peter as His friend and possibly led to his arrest. So Jesus selflessly sent a nonverbal message via eye contact: *Peter, look at Me. I forgave you before you even denied Me. I just want you to know that I haven't given up on you. We're still in this thing together!*

THE EVIDENCE AGAINST US

It is difficult for us to comprehend something we are incapable of. And the unmerited grace of God might top the list. The best way to understand the grace of God is not through left-brain analysis. That's too pixelated. The best way to understand the grace of God is through right-brain pictures. And Peter's repeated failures give us three-dimensional pictures of God's grace.

Peter's impulsiveness led to a lot of moments of vulnerability. One of them happened just a few hours before his denial. When the religious mob came to arrest Jesus, Peter pulled out a sword and cut off the ear of a man named Malchus. Peter gets a bum rap for his reaction, but you've got to give him credit. I don't see any of the other disciples coming to Jesus' defense!

Now let me state the obvious: you don't cut off someone's ear and get away with it, especially if that someone is the servant of the high priest. Peter was in a world of legal trouble. Worst-case scenario, Peter would get charged with attempted murder. Best-case scenario, Peter would get charged with assault and battery with a deadly weapon. But either way, Peter was going to serve some jail time.

We tend to ignore this subplot in the story, but it is one of the clearest pictures of grace in the gospels. Jesus miraculously reversed the irreversible by reattaching the man's amputated ear. But He did more than heal someone who had come to crucify Him; He also destroyed the evidence against Peter.

Stop and think about it. Malchus files suit against Peter, and a stenographer captures the cross-examination.

Malchus says, "Peter cut off my ear."

"Which ear?" the judge asks.

Malchus says, "My right one."[82]

The judge walks over to the witness stand and examines the ear. "It looks fine to me." And the case gets thrown out of court for lack of evidence!

Through His crucifixion and resurrection, Jesus destroyed the evidence against us.[83] But He did more than that. Not only does our sin get paid for out of His account, but all of His righteousness gets credited to our account. "God made him who had no sin to be sin for us, so that in him we might become the righteousness of God."[84] It's like Jesus says, "You give Me all of your sin. I'll give you all of My righteousness. And we'll call it even."

Nothing is more amazing to me than the spiritual transaction that takes place when we put our faith in Christ. Somehow my spiritual debits are transferred to Christ's account and His credits are transferred to mine. What a deal! There is no greater moment and no greater feeling than all of our guilt meeting all of God's grace.

GUILTY SECRETS

Do you remember what Adam did after he ate from the Tree of the Knowledge of Good and Evil? For the first time in his life, Adam hid from God.[85] It's comical when you think about it. Is anything more futile than trying to hide from the All-Seeing Eye? But that is what we do. We hide from God. And we hide from each other. Hiding after sinning is the first conditioned reflex recorded in Scripture, and not much has changed. We try to hide our sin and end up in a cage of guilt.

When I was in high school, I got pulled over by the police a grand total of thirteen times. I'm not proud of that statistic, but I am proud of this: I only got three tickets. I was a terrible driver—but I was a pretty good talker!

I got my first ticket on the way to a basketball game. I made a left-hand turn at a forty-five-degree angle into oncoming traffic that would have made NASCAR fans proud. The police officer I cut off? Not so much! She did a U-turn and wrote me a fifty-dollar ticket. That doesn't seem like much now, but it was a small fortune to me then. I had no idea how I was going to pay for it. But I decided to keep the ticket a secret and try to pay for it myself.

Like any good son, I was concerned about my parents' psychological well-being and didn't want to worry them with what I'd done wrong. But I made one error in judgment. I didn't realize that the police department (who probably knew there were lots of good kids just like me who didn't want their parents to worry) sent a copy of the ticket to my home address. Listen, when your mom sees a letter from the police department addressed to her son, red flags go up and she's probably going to open it. My mom showed it to my dad without me knowing they knew. And they kept my secret a secret.

Meanwhile, I lived under a cloud of guilt. I felt bad about keeping the ticket a secret, but the longer I kept the secret, the harder it was to come clean. I also lived in constant fear that my parents would somehow find out. And to top it off, I felt the financial pressure of trying to come up with fifty bucks to pay for the ticket.

Several weeks passed, and the last game of the regular season rolled around. Thousands of people packed the stands as we played our crosstown rivals for the conference championship. It was the most important and most memorable game of my high school basketball career. The Naperville Central Redskins staged one of the greatest comebacks I've ever been a part of. With five minutes left in the fourth quarter, we were down by twenty-one points. That's an insurmountable deficit by high school standards, but we came back to beat the Naperville North Huskies in OT. At the final buzzer, our fans flooded the court and it was complete euphoria.

That's when my dad came on the court and told me that he was going to pay for the ticket. I don't know why he chose that moment. I didn't even know he knew about the ticket. But I'll never forget the mixture of emotions I experienced. There was certainly a twinge of guilt because my sins had found me out, but I also remember the overwhelming sense of relief. It felt even better than the victory! I didn't have to pay for the ticket. And more important, I didn't have to live in fear anymore because my secret was out in the open.

Nothing is as freeing as confessed sin. Nothing is as isolating as a guilty secret. And that is why the Enemy wants you to keep your sins a secret. If you keep your sins a secret, you will be trapped in the cage of guilt the rest of your life. The only way out is confession. And I don't just mean confession to God. I certainly believe that we are completely forgiven when we confess our sin to God.[86] But confessing our sins to one another may be the least-practiced spiritual discipline in Scripture.[87] You know why you need to confess your sin? It's not just to ease your guilty conscience. You need to confess so that the person you're confessing to knows that they aren't alone.

THE JOHARI WINDOW

When I was in graduate school, I was introduced to a fascinating matrix on human personality called the Johari window. It is made up of four quadrants. The *arena quadrant* consists of those things you know about you and others know about you. It is your public persona. The *blind-spot quadrant* consists of those things others know about you but you don't know about you. This is where you need friends who have the courage to confront. The *facade quadrant* consists of those things you know about you but others don't know about you. This is where you hide who you really are. And the *unknown quadrant* consists of those things you don't know about you and others don't know about you. This is where the Holy Spirit plays a vital role in your life. God knows you better than you know yourself. So if you really want to get to know who you are, you've got to get to know God.

I'm concerned that many Christians get stuck in the facade quadrant. Let's be honest, the church can be the most pretentious place on earth. We're afraid of revealing our imperfections and dysfunctions. We're afraid of revealing our painful scars and sinful secrets. And that is why so many people are so lonely.

I've met many people who feel like they have to get their act together before coming to God. Where did that ludicrous logic come from? That's like suggesting you have to get healthy before going to see a doctor. It makes no sense.[88] The church needs to be a safe place where we can reveal our worst sins. Anything less is hypocrisy.

Over my years as a pastor, I've heard lots of confessions. And some of them have been shocking. I've had people who seem to be models of holiness come and confess everything from addiction to adultery. And I used to be surprised. But I'm not surprised anymore. You know what surprises me now? Someone who has the courage to confess. That's shocking! And my level of respect for the person confessing, no matter how bad the sin may seem, always goes up. Why? Because all of us have guilty secrets, but it takes a courageous person to confess.

You may feel as if your life would end if you were to make a confession or admit an addiction. That is the moment your life will begin. Confession opens the cage. And the spiritual adventure begins. You no longer have to expend lots of emotional and spiritual energy trying to hide who you really are. Your guilty conscience is set free to guide you. And you can quit pretending to be who you're not and start trying to become who God has called you to be.

RECOMMISSIONED

"I'm going out to fish."[89] Several weeks after his denial, Peter made this proclamation. And I suppose it's possible that Peter just wanted to go fishing. But part of me wonders if postdenial Peter thought his career as a disciple was over. Wouldn't you? Peter had failed one too many times. Maybe Peter was thinking about going back to fishing for a living. That is our natural inclination when we experience failure, isn't it? We revert to our old ways. And Satan would have loved nothing more than for Peter to have spent the rest of his life in a fishing boat on the Sea of Galilee. But Peter was commissioned by Christ to go to the ends of the earth proclaiming the good news.

Guilt has a shrinking effect. It shrinks our dreams. It shrinks our relationships. It shrinks our hearts. It shrinks our lives to the size of our greatest failures.

Grace has the opposite effect. It expands our dreams. It expands our relationships. It expands our hearts. And it gives us the courage to chase the Wild Goose all the way to the ends of the earth.

Postdenial Peter had been living in his cage of guilt for several weeks when he was recommissioned by post-Resurrection Jesus. And the way it happened was no coincidence.

> Jesus said to Simon Peter, "Simon son of John, do you truly love me more than these?"
>
> "Yes, Lord," he said, "you know that I love you."
>
> Jesus said, "Feed my lambs."
>
> Again Jesus said, "Simon son of John, do you truly love me?"
>
> He answered, "Yes, Lord, you know that I love you."
>
> Jesus said, "Take care of my sheep."
>
> The third time he said to him, "Simon son of John, do you love me?"
>
> Peter was hurt because Jesus asked him the third time, "Do you love me?" He said, "Lord, you know all things; you know that I love you."
>
> Jesus said, "Feed my sheep."[90]

I don't think it's any coincidence that Jesus asked Peter the same question three times. Peter was insulted by the repetition. But is it possible that Jesus knew a little something about conditioned reflexes long before Ivan Pavlov came along? Peter failed three times; Jesus recommissioned him three times. But that's not all. Have you ever noticed *when* the recommissioning took place? "Early in the morning."[91]

Jesus reconditioned Peter while the roosters were crowing. From that moment forward, the rooster's crow was no longer a reminder of his failure that produced feelings of guilt. It was a reminder of his recommissioning that produced feelings of gratitude.

Think of it this way:

Sin − Grace = Guilt
Sin + Grace = Gratitude

The grace of God is the difference between drowning in guilt and swimming in gratitude. When your spiritual reflexes have been reconditioned by the grace of God, it frees you up to come out of the cage of guilt and chase the Wild Goose.

YOUR CHASE

- What is the "rooster's crow" that sets off guilty feelings inside you?
- This chapter states, "So many people are prisoners to one or two or three experiences in their past." What are those one or two or three experiences for *you*?

⊛ Who do you need to forgive in order to be free to follow the Wild Goose? Who do you need to ask to forgive you?

⊛ Assuming you are a follower of Jesus, I'm sure you *understand* that He has given you His righteousness in exchange for your sin. But would you say that you really *feel* that the transaction has happened—and *live* as if it's true? Why or why not?

⊛ If you could see Jesus face to face and ask Him to recommission you, freeing you from your guilt and freeing you to follow Him, what would you say to Him?

CHAPTER 6

Sometimes It Takes a Shipwreck

Coming Out of the Cage of Failure

If you want to make God laugh, tell him your plans.

—John Chancellor

L ike everyone else, I have my fair share of bad days. But I can honestly say that I wouldn't want to be anyplace else doing anything else. I love pastoring National Community Church. I love living on Capitol Hill. And I pray for the privilege of pastoring one church for life. But here's the rest of the story: if it weren't for a ship-wreck in Chicago, I never would have landed in Washington DC in the first place.

When I was in seminary, I dreamed of planting a church in the Chicago area. My wife and I both grew up in Naperville, a western suburb. I love Chicago-style pizza. And back then Michael Jordan was still playing for the Chicago Bulls. Why would anyone want to move? (Besides the fifty-below windchill during winter, of course.) I thought we would live there the rest of our lives. So we formed a core group, opened a bank account, and chose a church name. I even put together a twenty-five-year strategic plan.

In retrospect, I wonder if God was chuckling while I was planning. Because we never even had our first service. Our plans fell apart before we could get the church plant off the ground. Actually, it was our core group that fell apart. It was during some crisis counseling with one of the couples in our core group that I realized the dream was imploding. Our core group fell apart and so did my twenty-five-year plan.

That failed attempt at church planting still ranks as one of the most embarrassing and disillusioning seasons of my life. But I wouldn't trade it for anything. Failure handled improperly can be devastating, but failure handled properly is the best thing that can happen to us. Failure teaches us our most valuable lessons. It keeps us from taking the credit for or taking for granted later successes. We make the all-important discovery that even when we fall flat on our faces, God is right there to pick us back up again. And failure also has a way of opening us up to other options.

When the dream of planting a church in Chicago died, I was willing to go wherever the Wild Goose wanted to take me. And honestly, the farther from Chicago the better! But I'm not sure I would have been open to moving to DC if the ship hadn't sunk in Chicago.

I still have lots of unanswered questions about that church plant. Were we even called to plant the church in the first place? Or did

God plan the failure? Was our timing off? Or was it my ineptitude that caused it to sink? I have more questions than answers, but I came out of the experience with a new conviction: sometimes it takes a shipwreck to get us where God wants us to go.

I believe in planning. Failing to plan is planning to fail. But when we trust our plans more than we trust God, our plans can keep us from pursuing Him and His will. And sometimes our plans have to fail in order for God's plans to succeed.

Failure (or what at the time looks like failure) can become a cage if you let it. It can keep you from pursuing the passions God has placed in your heart. But there's life after failure. The door of the cage swings open, and the Wild Goose calls you to a life of new adventures.

Enter Paul.

BAD LUCK CLUB

Toward the end of his missionary career, Paul was on his way to Rome to stand trial before Caesar when his ship sank in the Mediterranean Sea.

The closest I've ever come to a shipwreck was in the Galápagos. Despite large doses of Dramamine, most of us lost our lunch. There were tense moments when ocean waves tipped our boat at unbelievable angles. And let me state for the record: drowning at sea ranks right at the top of the list of ways I do not want to die.

I'm not exactly sure what Paul was thinking or feeling as the ship went down, but he had to be nauseous and anxious. The adrenaline must have been pumping as he tried to keep his head above water. And he had to be emotionally and physically drained when he finally

made it to shore. But before Paul could even dry off, his day went
from bad to worse.

> Once we were safe on shore, we learned that we were on the
> island of Malta. The people of the island were very kind to
> us. It was cold and rainy, so they built a fire on the shore to
> welcome us and warm us.
>
>   As Paul gathered an armful of sticks and was laying them
> on the fire, a poisonous snake, driven out by the heat, bit him
> on the hand. The people of the island saw it hanging from his
> hand and said to each other, "A murderer, no doubt! Though
> he escaped the sea, justice will not permit him to live."[92]

What a redefinition of what it means to have a bad day! A shipwreck alone qualifies as a bad day. But a shipwreck *and* a snakebite?
That is a terrible, horrible, no good, very bad day. If I'm making up
the rules, a shipwreck and snakebite in the same day earns you a lifetime membership in the Bad Luck Club.

If I were Paul, I would have been throwing my arms in the air at
this point. "Come on, God. If I was going to get bitten by a poiso-
nous snake, why didn't You just let me drown?" But God has a way
of turning what seems like bad luck into a big break. He turns shipwrecks and snakebites into supernatural synchronicities that somehow serve His purposes.

> Paul shook off the snake into the fire and was unharmed.
> The people waited for him to swell up or suddenly drop
> dead. But when they had waited a long time and saw that

he wasn't harmed, they changed their minds and decided he was a god.

Near the shore where we landed was an estate belonging to Publius, the chief official of the island. He welcomed us and treated us kindly for three days. As it happened, Publius's father was ill with fever and dysentery. Paul went in and prayed for him, and laying his hands on him, he healed him. Then all the other sick people on the island came and were healed. As a result we were showered with honors, and when the time came to sail, people supplied us with everything we would need for the trip.[93]

Let me state the obvious: Paul and Publius never should have met. Malta wasn't even on Paul's itinerary. And if Paul, a prisoner of the Imperial Regiment, had requested an audience with the chief official of Malta, I'm guessing he would have been laughed off the island. It took a shipwreck to strategically position Paul at this exact latitude and longitude: 35°50′ N, 14°35′ E. And it took a snakebite to set up this divine appointment with Publius. The shipwreck and snakebite were certainly not part of Paul's plan. But when you chase the Wild Goose, you never know where you'll go or who you'll meet. He may just use a shipwreck and a snakebite to set up an islandwide revival.

Only God!

DIVINE DETOURS

To me, some of the most enlightening and inspiring parts of the Bible aren't even in the Bible. They are in the appendix. Turn to the

back of a study Bible and look at the maps of Paul's missionary jour-
neys. Or should I say Wild Goose chases? Nary a straight line. Paul
zigzagged all over the ancient world.

If you read the account of his travels in the book of Acts, you
discover that some of Paul's destinations were planned. But many of
them weren't even on the itinerary. Paul ended up in Athens because
a Jewish mob in Thessalonica ran him out of town. He traveled to
Troas because the Holy Spirit closed the door to Bithynia. And Paul
landed on Malta because his ship sank in the Mediterranean. Athens,
Troas, and Malta weren't part of his plan. But God used what seemed
like detours to position Paul right where He wanted him.

I'm certainly not suggesting that you sabotage yourself. Don't
incite a mob or put a hole in the bottom of your boat. But sometimes a closed door is the very thing that gets us where God wants
us to go. I've come to think of closed doors as divine detours. And
while our failed plans can be incredibly discouraging and disorienting, God often uses the things that seem to be taking us off our
course to keep us on *His* course.

When it became painfully obvious that our church plant in
Chicago wasn't going to happen, my head started spinning. I had no
idea where to go or what to do. It was an awkward place emotionally and spiritually. And I dreaded the inevitable question—"What
are you going to do when you graduate?"—because I had no clue
what to do. I actually enrolled in a second master's degree program
just to buy some time.

Few things are as disorienting as in-between times—between
jobs, between relationships, or between a rock and a hard place. But

nothing rattles the cage like a bad diagnosis, a pink slip, or divorce papers. They cause the compass needle to spin. And we feel lost because our plans and our lives fall apart. But the upside is that it causes us to seek God with a raw intensity that cannot be manufactured any other way. Disorientation has a way of driving us to our knees. And that is one reason why the bad things that happen to us can actually turn into the best things that happen to us.

TRAGEDY OR COMEDY?

How we handle the shipwrecks in our lives will determine whether our lives become a tragedy or comedy. We can't control what happens to us. But we can control our response.

Not long ago I got an e-mail from an NCCer whose compass needle was spinning. Political scandals are par for the course in DC, and the rest of the nation hears about them on the news and then conveniently flips the channel. But those scandals touch the people I pastor in a personal way.

> I've found myself in a surreal world over the last few months. After being in DC for less than three years and having already switched jobs three times, I crazily accepted another change of scenery this last spring to work for a well-respected senator from my home state. The world of the Hill is an odd beast. Add to the plate of a clueless staffer a piece of major legislation moving on my watch, and I thought things were as fun and stressful and wonderful as they could be. But add to that

a vicious national media blitz involving my boss, and all of
a sudden my world morphs into tragedy in a matter of one
news cycle.

I suppose it wouldn't have been such a painful and
exhausting experience if I didn't have (and continue to have)
such great respect for my boss. I chose to stay with him
through all this and in doing so subjected myself to the worst
side of both politics and human nature. I saw him be ruthlessly
and wrongly dragged through the mud, kicked, scorned, and
run over time and time again. So as much as I still want to join
a kick-boxing class to take out my daily political and career
frustrations, I wanted to cry "Tragedy!" from the rooftops.

Have you ever felt like your life was turning into a tragedy? A
spouse cheats on you. A boss unfairly fires you. Or someone hurts
you in a way that seems beyond your ability to heal.

Listen, you still get to choose your attitude. And while you may
not like the chapter of life you're in, the final chapter has yet to be
written. I like this NCCer's response when it seemed as if the ship
were sinking.

I don't have a clue about what God will be authoring on
tomorrow's page, but of the end I'm sure. So it is my choice
to claim tragedy or comedy for today. I actually feel a bit like
I'm in a Choose Your Own Adventure book (do kids still read
those?), and God is getting a kick out of yanking me through
as many different scenarios as possible—ridden with tragedy
and comedy alike—so I have no choice but to focus on His

masterfully designed fairy-tale ending. Bottom line...right
now He's working on morphing this current tragedy into a
comedy, all the while teaching me to live even stronger in the
inspiration of the fairy tale.

If you feel like you're stuck in a tragedy, here's my advice: give
Jesus complete editorial control over your life. You have to quit trying to write your own story. And you need to accept Jesus not only
as Lord and Savior but also as Author. If you allow Him to begin
writing His-story through your life, it'll give the tragedy a fairy-tale
ending. I'm not promising a life without heartache or pain or loss,
but I am promising a different ending.

If you want a glimpse of what God can do, consider the story of
the criminals who were crucified with Jesus. One criminal hurled
insults at Jesus. "But the other criminal rebuked him. 'Don't you fear
God,' he said, 'since you are under the same sentence? We are pun-
ished justly, for we are getting what our deeds deserve. But this man
has done nothing wrong.' "[94]

Who wants his story to end hanging on a cross for the crimes he
has committed? Can you imagine a more tragic ending to a human
life than death by crucifixion? This is the worst day and last day of
his life. But the story wasn't quite over. The last sentence had not yet
been written. And at the last moment, the repentant criminal
reached out to the Man on the middle cross: "Jesus, remember me
when you come into your kingdom." It's one of the simplest profes-
sions of faith recorded in the gospels. And Jesus turns the worst day
and last day of his life into the best day and first day of the rest of
eternity: "Today you will be with me in paradise."[95]

If that isn't a happily-ever-after ending, I don't know what is. But let me say this point-blank: the ending to your story is entirely contingent on whether you turn to Jesus the way this criminal on the cross turned to Him. If you don't, the tragedy remains a tragedy. If you do, the tragedy ends and the fairy tale begins.

Again, I'm not promising a perfect life. Jesus Himself said, "In this world you will have trouble."[96] Bad things happen to good people. You will experience some shipwrecks and snakebites along the way. But when you give Jesus complete editorial control over your life, He begins writing His-story through your life.

TOTAL DEPENDENCE

In normal human relationships we move along a continuum from total dependence to total independence. Babies cannot do anything for themselves. They are totally dependent upon their parents to feed them, burp them, rock them, and change them. And our goal as parents is to move our children toward total independence, especially with the potty-training part. For what it's worth, the word *diaper* spelled backward is *repaid.*

A healthy relationship between parent and child moves from dependence to independence. But a healthy relationship with our heavenly Father moves in the opposite direction. Spiritually speaking, we start out in a state of total independence. Sin is living life independently of God. It is living as if God does not exist. It is saying to God, "Thanks but no thanks; I'm going to try to make it on my own." Spiritual maturity is moving along the continuum toward total dependence on God. It is saying to God, "I'll take all the help

I can get." It is learning to live in daily dependence upon God. And sometimes it takes a shipwreck or a snakebite to get us there.

Disorientation is natural and healthy. It is a normal part of chasing the Wild Goose. We won't know exactly where we're going much of the time, but that disorientation develops our dependence upon God. And it is our dependence upon God, not our best-laid plans, that will get us where God wants us to go.

New chapters in our lives often begin with an orientation. You go through an orientation when you start at a new school or get a new job. But God begins new chapters in our lives via disorientation. Jesus didn't do orientations. Jesus did disorientations. Doesn't it seem like His disciples were in a constant state of disorientation? We think it's because of their spiritual immaturity, but maybe it models the way God makes disciples. Sometimes God needs to disorient us so He can reorient us.

One thing I know is this: if it weren't for some disorientation in Chicago, I never would have been reoriented toward Washington DC.

Thank God for failed plans!

A Sense of Destiny

The church I serve as pastor, National Community Church, may be one of the most disoriented churches in the country. That's because 70 percent of NCCers are single twentysomethings who are navigating the quarterlife crisis.

The third decade of life is full of spiritual, relational, occupational, and even geographical disorientation. Twentysomethings are making the decisions they will manage the rest of their lives. *What do I believe? Who should I marry? What should I do with my life? Where should I live?* Those are tough decisions with lifelong ramifications. And that is why the quarterlife crisis can be so disorienting.

My cousin-in-law Dave Schmidgall was navigating some of those quarterlife issues a few years ago when we invited him over for dinner to talk through some of the decisions he was trying to make. He was experiencing disorientation on all fronts. He wasn't sure what to do with his degree. He loved living in DC, but he was thinking about moving back home. And he wasn't sure where his relationship with his girlfriend would or should go. We talked for several hours. Then I prayed one of those unscripted prayers where you aren't sure exactly what you're saying until after you've said it. "Lord, thank You that You want us to get where You want us to go more than we want to get where You want us to go."

We actually quit praying and started laughing when those words came out of my mouth because we weren't sure what I had just prayed. It took a minute to decipher the riddle, but once we did, we felt a tremendous sense of relief. All the stress was taken off our shoulders when we reminded ourselves of this simple truth: God is far more concerned about your future than you are.

We put so much pressure on ourselves, as if the eternal plans of almighty God are contingent upon our ability to decipher them. The truth is, God wants to reveal them more than we want to know them. And if we think one misstep can frustrate the providential plans of the Omnipotent One, then our God is way too small. Not only does God want us to get where God wants us to go more than we want to get where God wants us to go, but He is awfully good at getting us there. He may not always reveal His plans how or when we want Him to. But when we chase the Wild Goose, our future becomes His responsibility. "In his heart a man plans his course, but the LORD determines his steps."[97]

Do me a favor. Stop reading for a moment and take a deep breath. Now let it out.

A deep breath recalibrates us physiologically. It relaxes us. The sovereignty of God has the same effect on me spiritually. When I'm reminded that God is the one ordering my footsteps, it helps me relax. God is in the business of positioning us in the right place at the right time. And that ought to give us an unshakeable sense of destiny even when we feel disoriented.

DIVINE APPOINTMENTS

A few years ago I was leafing through connection cards after one of our weekend services, and one of them caught my attention. Next to the question asking guests how they had heard about National Community Church, someone had written "Blockbuster." That was a first.

A few weeks earlier I had been in line at our neighborhood Blockbuster, and the woman standing next to me asked what time it was. She noticed the church logo on my watch, and we struck up a conversation. I discovered that she was dechurched, so I invited her to check out NCC some weekend.

She sent me an e-mail after her first visit:

We met at the Blockbuster video at Hechinger Mall a few weeks ago. I made a comment about what an interesting watch you were wearing. I just wanted you to know that last Sunday

I felt compelled to be at National Community Church, and it was everything I needed to hear. Your message on Sunday changed my entire life and mind-set. I sincerely believe it was a divine appointment. I'm glad I did not let anything keep me from coming. I said to someone a couple months ago, "I'm all churched out." But I'm looking forward to church this Sunday, and I haven't been able to say that in a long time!

Sometimes my imagination gets carried away, but I envision an entire department of angels devoted to divine appointments. This woman was on the agenda because she was *all churched out*. And it may be wishful thinking on my part, but one of the angels recommends National Community Church. Our names are cross-checked in an angelic database and a strategy is devised. *There is only one way they're going to cross paths because there is only one thing they have in common. Both of them love movies, and both of them are members of the Blockbuster at Hechinger Mall. And make sure Mark wears his watch!*

Voilà!

I don't know if that's exactly how it goes down. But I do know this: God is setting up divine appointments all the time. And as long as our motives stay pure and our spirits stay sensitive, He will make sure we meet the right people at the right time. And that ought to buoy our spirits even when it feels like the ship is sinking!

I pray for divine appointments all the time. And I make no apologies for it. In fact, I remember specifically praying for divine appointments before heading to the Galápagos with a team of NCCers. And God answered those prayers in dramatic fashion.

On our last day we got up early for a forty-five-minute bus trip across the island of Santa Cruz to catch an airport ferry to a neigh-boring island. There was only one paved road between the port city and the ferry, with virtually no civilization in between. In the mid-dle of the island, in the middle of nowhere, we were surprised to see a hitchhiker standing by the side of the road. I probably would have waved and kept on driving, but our bus driver pulled over and picked up a middle-aged islander named Raul. He was unshaven. It looked as if he had been walking for hours. And it was obvious he hadn't gotten much sleep the night before.

Raul could have taken a seat anywhere on the bus, but God sat him right next to Adam. Adam is one of the friendliest and most car-ing people I know. He was also one of the few people on our team who spoke fluent Spanish. And despite his own pain due to a C11 compression fracture from cliff jumping the day before, Adam sensed a divine appointment.

In the course of their conversation, Raul told Adam that he had tried to commit suicide the day before. He tied cinder blocks around his ankles and planned on throwing himself into the ocean because his wife of thirty years had left him. Adam didn't just understand what he said; he understood how he felt. Only a few years before, Adam's wife of fifteen years had left him and he too had been suicidal.

Raul told Adam that he felt like God was never there for him, but he had to admit that God was looking out for him on August 12, 2006. Raul finally found the God who had been chasing him his entire life.

On a human plane, there is no way we should have met Raul. You cannot manufacture those kinds of meetings. We live in differ-ent countries and speak different languages. We were separated by several plane rides, bus rides, and boat rides. But God knows no spatial or chronological limitations. Setting up a divine appointment in a different hemisphere is as simple for God as setting up a divine appointment with your next-door neighbor.

ON A DIME

When you chase the Wild Goose, life can turn on a dime. You never know how or where the Holy Spirit is going to reveal His plans. One trip, one meeting, one article, one class, one conversation can radically change the trajectory of your life. Or in my case, one magazine advertisement.

I don't even remember what magazine I was reading. But I was sitting at our kitchen table eating lunch and leafing through the pages of the magazine when I came across an advertisement for a parachurch ministry in Washington DC. I'm not even sure why I stopped flipping pages. I had never been to DC. And the parachurch ministry wasn't what I was looking for. But I felt prompted to make a phone call. That phone call led to a trip. And that trip led to a cross-country move. Within a few months, Lora and I had packed all our earthly belongings into a U-Haul truck and made the move to Washington DC. We had no place to live and no guaranteed salary, but we knew DC was the next stop on the Wild Goose chase.

The longer I chase the Wild Goose, the more I appreciate this simple truth: our reasons and God's reasons are often very different. I thought I was moving to DC to direct a parachurch ministry, but

God had ulterior motives. He had reasons that I was totally unaware of because I'm not omniscient. God didn't call me to Washington DC to direct a parachurch ministry. Sure, I did that for a while. But I'm convinced that the Wild Goose led me to Washington DC to pastor National Community Church even though National Community Church didn't exist yet. God always has reasons that we are unaware of.

WIND FACTOR

How did Paul end up on the island of Malta? It wasn't because of the navigational skills of the ship's captain. It wasn't because of the sailing skills of the crew. They landed on Malta because of something that was totally out of their control: the wind factor.

They encountered headwinds that made it difficult to keep the ship on course.

The wind was against them, so they sailed down to the leeward side of Crete.

A light wind began blowing from the south.

They couldn't turn the ship into the wind.

Gale-force winds continued to batter the ship.[98]

You get the point. The wind seemed to be taking them off course, but it was the wind factor that got Paul right where God wanted him to go.

Not long ago I was on a flight that was grounded because of high winds. The pilot informed us that, because of the airline's rules, he could not take off if the wind was blowing at thirty knots or more. And as we sat on the tarmac, I couldn't help but consider the incongruity of the situation. We were sitting in a Boeing 737 aircraft with twin CFM56-3-B2 engines that would defy the law of gravity and power us to a cruising speed of 509 mph. But there wasn't a thing we could do about the wind. Wind is unpredictable and uncontrollable. You can't stop it from blowing. You can't change the direction it is blowing. Wind will be wind.

What does that remind you of? "The wind blows wherever it pleases. You hear its sound, but you cannot tell where it comes from or where it is going. So it is with everyone born of the Spirit."[99]

Jesus likened the working of the Holy Spirit to the wind. Sometimes the Spirit is a light wind from the south. Other times He is a gale-force wind that batters our ship. Sometimes the Spirit is a headwind that seems to frustrate our plans. And other times He is the wind at our back.

Chasing the Wild Goose is recognizing which way the wind of the Spirit is blowing and responding to it. It requires a moment-by-moment sensitivity to the Wild Goose. And you have to trust His promptings more than you trust your own plans. Instead of getting frustrated by fighting the wind, you appreciate the fact that something uncontrollable and unpredictable will get you where God wants you to go.

As I look back at the map of my own Wild Goose chase, I am grateful for the shipwrecks and snakebites. Sure, shipwrecks are scary and snakebites are painful. But I have no idea where I would be if it weren't for some divine detours along the way. It is the shipwrecks and snakebites that make us who we are. And they are the stories we love to tell later in life. How many times do you think Paul told *his* shipwreck and snakebite story?

Closed Doors

When our plans fail, it enables us to consider other options. And it often changes the trajectory of our lives. That is what happened early in our journey at National Community Church. We had been meeting in a DC public school for about a year when we were informed that the school was closing because of fire-code violations, effective immediately.

It felt like the ship would sink. We could easily have become a church planting statistic, and only a handful of people would have felt the difference. But God used that closed door to point us in another direction. I started looking at different rental options on Capitol Hill. And after knocking on about twenty-five different doors, the only one that opened was the movie theaters at Union Station. And what a door it was.

It is hard to imagine a more strategic spiritual beachhead than the movie theaters at Union Station, with its 25 million visitors every year. All I can say is this: thank God for closed doors! If God hadn't closed the door to the DC public school, I don't think we would have been looking for an open door at the theater.

On the day I signed the lease with the movie theater at Union Station, I picked up a book titled *Union Station: A History of Washington's Grand Terminal.* I wanted to know the story behind the station. And God used the history to give me a sense of destiny.

On February 28, 1903, President Theodore Roosevelt signed the congressional bill allowing for the creation of Union Station. The bill simply stated: "An Act of Congress to create a Union Station, and for other purposes."

It was that last phrase—"and for other purposes"—that jumped off the page and into my spirit. Theodore Roosevelt thought he was building a train station, but God had grander motives. God knew that a century after that bill was signed, Union Station would serve His purposes through the ministry of National Community Church.

And it all started with a closed door.

One of my favorite promises and frequent prayers is found in the book of Revelation. "These are the words of him who is holy and true, who holds the key of David. What he opens no one can shut, and what he shuts no one can open. I know your deeds. See, I have placed before you an open door that no one can shut."[100]

The key of David is an allusion to Eliakim, who held the highest position in Hezekiah's royal court. As mayor of the royal palace, Eliakim wore the key to the house of David around his shoulder. The key symbolized his authority. He was the only person in the palace who had access to every room. There was no door he could not shut. There was no door he could not open.[101]

Jesus now holds the key of David. What He shuts no one can open, and what He opens no one can shut. He is the Door.[102] And when you walk through the Door, you never know where you'll go, who you'll meet, or what you'll do. He is the God who opens doors for prisoners like Paul to have divine appointments with chief officials like Publius.

DIVINE DELAYS

I don't like delays and detours anymore than anyone else. I'm your typical Type A personality. I want to get where I want to go as quickly and easily as possible.

Every time the Batterson family sets out on a vacation, I have a road-trip ritual. I reset the mileage and elapsed time settings on our deluxe odometer; then I toggle between them the entire trip. My goal is simple: I want to set a new land-speed record anytime we go anywhere!

I tend to live the way I drive. I want to get from point A to point B in the shortest amount of time and by the easiest route possible. But I've come to realize that *getting where God wants me to go* isn't nearly as important as *becoming who God wants me to be* in the process. And God seems to be far less concerned with where I'm going than with who I'm becoming.

I think some of us want to know the will of God more than we want to know God. And it short-circuits spiritual growth. You can't do the will of God if you don't have the heart of God. And that is where shipwrecks and snakebites come into play. They don't just get us where God wants us to go; they help us become who He wants us to be.

As Oswald Chambers said,

We must never put our dreams of success as God's purpose for us. The question of getting to a particular end is a mere incident. What we call the process, God calls the end. His purpose is that I depend on Him and on His power now.

It is the process, not the end, which is glorifying
to God.[103]

In recent days, quite a few dreams have become reality. National
Community Church launched its fourth location in Georgetown.
AOL City Guide voted Ebenezers the number-two coffeehouse in
the metro DC area. And my first book, *In a Pit with a Lion on a
Snowy Day*, reached more readers than anyone expected. But none of
those dreams happened quickly or easily. There were lots of detours
and delays along the way.

There is nothing spectacular about the growth of National Community Church. It took nearly five years for us to grow from a core
group of 19 to 250 people. It took eight years of praying, negotiating,
rezoning, and building before the grand opening of Ebenezers. And
although I felt called to write when I was in seminary, it was more
than a decade before I landed a book contract with a publisher. It took
a long time for those dreams to become reality. And I am forever grateful that they did, because God taught me some invaluable lessons.

First, I've learned that *the longer the wait, the more you appreciate.* We take for granted those things we don't have to work for or
wait for. But hard work doubles as gratitude insurance. I don't take
our coffeehouse for granted. When I walk into Ebenezers, I understand that I am walking into a miracle. If it had taken half the time,
I would appreciate it half as much.

Second, I've learned that *sometimes the most spiritual thing you
can do is just hang in there.* There were times when I wished God had
not called me to write, because unfulfilled dreams are downright
depressing. There were times when I felt like throwing in the writing

towel, but when you feel like giving up or giving in, that is when you need to hang in there just a little bit longer. "He who began a good work in you will carry it on to completion."[104] And nothing builds emotional and spiritual endurance like divine delays.

Finally, I've learned that *a sense of humor can get you through just about anything*. As I look back, some of our greatest failures at NCC have turned into our funniest memories. When the church had about two hundred people in attendance, we brought in a band to do a concert, and I optimistically estimated that we'd have a hundred people attend. Only four people showed up. And there were seven people in the band! I've never wanted the Rapture to happen more than right before I had to go into the greenroom and tell the band that there were only four people out there. The whole night was awkward. What do you do when there are more people in the band than in the audience? Put the audience on the stage and put the band in the auditorium, where there's more room? It was awfully embarrassing at the time, but we have gotten more laughs out of that failed concert than you can imagine.

If you lose everything else, don't lose your sense of humor. A sense of humor can get you through just about anything. I'm convinced that the healthiest and holiest people are the people who laugh the most.

Enjoying the Journey

When I was in seminary, I interviewed for ministerial credentials, and one of the interviewers asked me a great question: "If you had to define yourself in one word, what would it be?"

Without a moment's hesitation, I said, "Driven." And I was proud of my answer then. I'm less proud of it now.

This is embarrassing to admit, but my original goal as a church planter was to pastor a thousand people before I turned thirty. All of us have subconscious definitions of success. That was mine. And there is nothing wrong with setting God-sized goals if the motive is right—the size of our dreams is a measure of our spiritual maturity. But the problem with that particular goal was that I was more concerned with the number than with the people. And besides that, all we can do is plant and water. God is the one who gives the increase.[105]

During our first year, I was often discouraged by our attendance. It wasn't uncommon to start our services with only six or eight people in attendance. I remember closing my eyes during worship because it was too depressing to open them. That is when I realized that my goal was a mirage. If I couldn't enjoy pastoring twenty-five people here and now, then I probably wouldn't enjoy pastoring a thousand people then and there. And I resolved two things. I resolved that I would be the best pastor I could be at every stage. And I resolved that I would enjoy the journey.

I don't know what detours your life has taken. I don't know what delays you have experienced. Maybe life has taken some unexpected turns. Maybe you feel like your dreams have been delayed or detoured. Life has not gone according to plan. I feel your frustration, and I empathize with your confusion. But that is the essence of adventure. The unpredictable twists and turns of life can drive you crazy. Or you can learn to enjoy the journey.

The choice is yours.

Dance Dance Revolution

A few years ago our entire staff was in Atlanta, Georgia. Every year we make the pilgrimage to the Catalyst Conference, and that year our team was at the airport waiting to catch a flight home. I was physically exhausted and couldn't wait to see my kids, but flights were delayed because of weather. The airport was packed. And everybody was a little frustrated. So our team decided to have some fun.

A few months earlier our staff had learned the *Napoleon Dynamite* dance and performed it at our annual variety show. So we decided to dust it off and do the dance. We turned Gate 10 into our stage and turned our fellow passengers into a captive audience. We actually got a nice round of applause, along with quite a few strange looks!

We were hoping we wouldn't see anybody we knew, since it is always easier embarrassing yourself in front of strangers. But a girl came up to us after the dance and told us she attended National Community Church. She was actually on the phone with another NCCer when we started dancing. She told her friend, "You won't believe it. Pastor Mark and the NCC staff are dancing in the middle of the Atlanta airport."

As I see it, you have two options when you don't like your circumstances: complain about them or make the most of them.

In the words of George Bernard Shaw, "People are always blaming their circumstances for what they are. I don't believe in circumstances. The people who get on in this world are the people who get up and look for the circumstances they want and if they can't find them, make them."

But it goes beyond that. You not only need to make the most of your circumstances; you also have to realize that God is in them. And He is capable of working them together for your good. It doesn't matter how long the delay or detour, He can make them work together for good. After all, shipwrecks and snakebites are His specialty.

YOUR CHASE

- ❀ Looking back on an event that disappointed you greatly at the time, what reasons can you see for God allowing the event to happen?
- ❀ Think of a "failure" you've experienced recently. In the plans of God, how might it turn out to be a detour instead of a dead end?
- ❀ How do you see the troubles, disappointments, and surprises of life transforming you into the person God wants you to be?
- ❀ Where are you in the School of Trusting God's Sovereignty? Entering high school? Working on your PhD dissertation? Still making paper chains in kindergarten?
- ❀ "The unpredictable twists and turns of life can drive you crazy. Or you can learn to enjoy the journey." Where are you at right now—insane or having an insane amount of fun?

CHAPTER 7

GOOD OLD-FASHIONED GUTS

Coming Out of the Cage of Fear

The price of our vitality is the sum of all our
fears.

—DAVID WHYTE

A pair of psychologists from the University of Michigan con-
ducted a fascinating study that sheds light on the fear of
loss.[106] Volunteers donned caps containing electrodes, and while they
engaged in a computer-simulated betting game, researchers analyzed
their brains' electrical activity in response to winning and losing. The
betting game allowed subjects to place either a five- or a twenty-five-
cent bet, and after they made their selection, the box they checked

turned green or red, indicating whether the bet was added to or subtracted from their winnings.

With each bet, the medial frontal cortex in their brains showed increased electrical activity within a matter of milliseconds. But what intrigued the researchers was that medial frontal negativity showed a larger dip after a loss than the rise in medial frontal positivity after a win. In fact, during a string of losses, medial frontal negativity dipped lower with each loss. So each loss was compounded by the previous loss. Researchers came to a simple yet profound conclusion: *losses loom larger than gains.* In other words, the aversion to loss of a certain magnitude is greater than the attraction to gain of the same magnitude.

Maybe that helps explain why so many people live their lives so defensively. Maybe that is why we fixate on sins of commission instead of sins of omission. And maybe that neurological tendency is one reason why many of us approach the will of God with a better-safe-than-sorry mentality. Instead of chasing the Wild Goose, we get trapped in the cage of fear, failing to pursue God passionately and find out what kind of adventure He has for us in building His kingdom.

Most of us are far too tentative when it comes to the will of God. We let our fears dictate our decisions. We are so afraid of making the wrong decision that we make no decision. And what we fail to realize is that indecision *is* a decision. And it is our indecision, not our bad decisions, that keeps us in the cage. Maybe we need to come to grips with another aphorism: nothing ventured, nothing gained.

What is most lacking in the church of Jesus Christ is not education or resources. Of course, we should keep learning, but most of us are educated way beyond the level of our obedience. And of course, we should keep giving, but we do not lack the resources to alleviate poverty or fight injustice or spread the gospel. We are the most resourced church in the most resourced country the world has ever known. You know what is most lacking? Good old-fashioned guts!

We need people who are more afraid of missing opportunities than making mistakes. People who are more afraid of lifelong regrets than temporary failure. People who dare to dream the unthinkable and attempt the impossible.

Enter Jonathan.

DARING PLANS

It happened in the early days of Saul's kingship, when the Philistines on the Israelites' western border threatened to destabilize the nation. Who would provide the bold action that was desperately needed?

> One day Jonathan son of Saul said to the young man bearing his armor, "Come, let's go over to the Philistine outpost on the other side." But he did not tell his father.
>
> Saul was staying on the outskirts of Gibeah under a pomegranate tree in Migron. With him were about six hundred men, among whom was Ahijah, who was wearing an ephod. He was a son of Ichabod's brother Ahitub son of Phinehas, the son of Eli, the LORD's priest in Shiloh. No one was aware that Jonathan had left.
>
> On each side of the pass that Jonathan intended to

cross to reach the Philistine outpost was a cliff; one was called Bozez, and the other Seneh. One cliff stood to the north toward Micmash, the other to the south toward Geba.

Jonathan said to his young armor-bearer, "Come, let's go over to the outpost of those uncircumcised fellows. Perhaps the LORD will act in our behalf. Nothing can hinder the LORD from saving, whether by many or by few."[107]

I'm not trying to psychoanalyze someone who lived thousands of years ago, but I think it is safe to say that Jonathan had a sanctified medial frontal cortex. He did not let his fears dictate his decisions. Jonathan played offense with his life. He courageously climbed the cliffs of Micmash and picked a fight with the Philistine army. And I love the way the New Living Translation captions the story: "Jonathan's Daring Plan."

To be honest, part of the reason I love Jonathan's daring plan is that it makes me feel better about my bad ideas. This has to be the worst military strategy I've ever heard of. Jonathan exposed himself to the Enemy in broad daylight. He conceded the high ground. And then he came up with this sign: "If [the Philistines] say, 'Come up to us,' we will climb up, because that will be our sign that the LORD has given them into our hands."[108]

I'm sorry, but if I were making up the signs, I would do the exact opposite. If they *come down to us,* that'll be our sign. Or better yet, if they *fall off the cliff,* that'll be our sign that the Lord is giving them into our hands. But no! Jonathan's plan was much more difficult, dangerous, and daring than that.

Have you ever climbed a cliff? I went rock climbing once, and my hands were clenched in a clawlike position for two hours after only twenty minutes of climbing. It was humbling and exhausting. Trust me, you don't want to go rock climbing before sword fighting. Besides that, there was no guarantee that Jonathan would even make it to the top. It's not like the Philistines threw down a rope. And to top it off, even if he made it to the top, Jonathan was seriously outnumbered by the Enemy, with no reinforcements and no retreat plan. This was a terrible battle plan, but you have to give Jonathan credit. It was definitely daring!

What motivated Jonathan to climb that cliff? Where did he get the guts? And how did he know it was God's will? It's impossible to know exactly what thoughts were in his mind, but one verse does reveal Jonathan's gestalt: "Perhaps the LORD will act in our behalf."[109]

I love that modus operandi. And I think it was the conviction that God would act on his behalf if he stepped out in faith that gave Jonathan the guts to climb the cliff.

Some of us have the opposite mode of operating: perhaps the Lord *won't* act in our behalf. We live out of fear instead of faith. And that lack of faith results in a lack of guts.

Jonathan did not wait for something to happen. He made something happen. He took action and did something daring. And that one daring decision was enough to shift the momentum and create a tipping point. "So the LORD rescued Israel that day."[110]

The will of God is *not* an insurance plan. The will of God is a daring plan! When was the last time you read the eleventh chapter of Hebrews? Not every story ends with seeming success. People were sawed in half, stoned to death, and chained in dungeons. But our Wild Goose chase doesn't end when we die. In fact, death is just the beginning. And it is that eternal perspective that gives us the courage to come out of the cage and live dangerously for the cause of Christ, even if it means death.

More often than not, the will of God will involve a daring decision that seems unsafe or even insane. But if you have the guts to climb the cliff, the Wild Goose will meet you at the top.

BLOOD-AND-GUTS

To celebrate a recent anniversary, Lora and I spent a few days in the Eternal City. Between long meals at sidewalk cafes, we visited historic sites around Rome where ancient Christians were persecuted for their faith before the emperor Constantine made Christianity the official religion of the Roman Empire in 313. We visited dungeons where Christians were imprisoned, coliseums where they were fed to wild animals for sport, and catacombs where they risked their lives to secretly worship God.

It is easy to forget where we come from, isn't it? I think *Foxe's Book of Martyrs* should be required reading for every twenty-first-century Christian living in a first-world country because most of us fail to fully appreciate the extreme sacrifices that were made and the courageous risks that were taken by our spiritual predecessors.

Consider Matthew's description of the early church. "The kingdom of heaven suffereth violence, and the violent take it by force."[111] In the first century, church was anything but a safe place. It was a dangerous place. But despite the persecution, the early church played offense. Another translation says, "From the days of John the Baptist until now, the kingdom of heaven has been forcefully advancing, and forceful men lay hold of it."[112]

There is nothing remotely passive about being part of the kingdom of God. We are called to forcefully advance the cause of Christ. Faithfulness is *not* holding the fort. Faithfulness is storming the gates of hell.

I've been inspired by a group of early-twentieth-century missionaries who became known as "one-way missionaries" because they packed all their earthly belongings into coffins and purchased one-way tickets when they departed for the mission field. They knew they'd never return home. The story is told of one such missionary named A. W. Milne who felt called to a tribe of headhunters in the New Hebrides. All the other missionaries to this tribe had been martyred, but that didn't keep Milne from chasing the Wild Goose. He lived among the tribe for thirty-five years and never returned home. When the tribe buried him, they wrote the following epitaph on his tombstone: "When he came there was no light. When he left there was no darkness."

When did we start believing that God wants to send us to safe places to do easy things? God wants to send us to dangerous places to do difficult things. And if you chase the Wild Goose, He will lead you into the shadowlands, where light and darkness clash.

Dare I suggest that the twenty-first-century church needs more daring people with daring plans?

My friend Mike Foster chased the Wild Goose to a dark place a few years ago. Mike was deeply concerned about the effect pornography was having on American culture, so he decided to infiltrate the adult film industry with the love of Christ and hand out "Jesus Loves Porn Stars" Bibles at porn conventions. Talk about a daring plan. It took good old-fashioned guts for Mike to take a stand for the sanctity of sex. As he was setting up the XXXchurch.com booth at his first porn show in Las Vegas, a thought ran through his head: *What am I doing here?*

Permission to speak frankly? If we are going to fulfill our ancient commission, we need to get out of the comfortable confines of our Christian ghettos and invade some hellholes with the light and love of Christ. That is exactly what Mike did, and thousands of porn addicts have found freedom and forgiveness as a result.

In the words of another daring twentieth-century missionary, C. T. Studd, "Some want to live within the sound of church or chapel bell; I want to run a rescue shop within a yard of hell." The church needs more Studds! And you can quote me on that.

THE HARD WAY

I think we've made a false assumption about the will of God. We subconsciously think it should get easier the longer we follow Christ. Let me push back a little. I certainly believe that some dimensions of spiritual growth get easier with the consistent practice of spiritual disciplines. But I also believe that spiritual growth prepares us for more dangerous missions. As we grow, God gives us more difficult things to do.

National Community Church launched its fourth location in Georgetown this past year. But Georgetown wasn't our first choice. When we started doing reconnaissance, we naturally and mindlessly looked for what we thought would be the easiest place to launch a location, and that definitely wasn't Georgetown. I don't want to exaggerate the challenge, but I have a friend who pastors a church in the Georgetown area who calls it "a graveyard for church planters" because so many church-plant attempts have failed to take root there. It is some of the toughest soil in DC. But after months of praying, some closed doors, and one God-ordained dream, we came to the conclusion that the path of least resistance was the wrong route for us. I'm not saying we shouldn't plant churches where we can expect the greatest growth, but sometimes God calls us to something more difficult or someplace more dangerous.

Rarely does the Holy Spirit lead us down the path of least resistance. It's not in His nature. To adapt a line from Robert Frost, your Wild Goose chase will probably take you down the road less traveled. You will have to climb a cliff or pick a fight with the Enemy. But you will discover this simple truth: the hard way is the best way.

Let me compare and contrast two days in the life of Mark Batterson.

Not long ago, our family was at the mall getting our kids haircuts at Cartoon Cuts, and on the way out we passed a Brookstone. I love shopping at Brookstone. I don't know if I've ever actually purchased anything there, but their massage chairs are amazing. On this particular day it was like the stars had aligned, because all five massage chairs were empty. So our entire clan spent fifteen minutes "shopping" at Brookstone. And to top it off, the store was playing an *80s Forever* CD. It doesn't get much better than that.

Everybody enjoys a little R and R now and then. And there is nothing wrong with lounging in a massage chair. But is that what makes life worth living? Stop and think about. What are your most cherished memories? They're not the easy victories or small challenges, are they? The greatest memories are of the toughest victories and biggest challenges. The most satisfying days are not the days when you had nothing to do. The most satisfying days are the hardest days—the days when you had everything to do and you did it.

A few years ago I was part of a team that spent a week doing humanitarian and missions work in Addis Ababa, the capital city of Ethiopia. One of the projects was building a mud hut for a hunchbacked, wrinkled grandmother who had lived most of her life in a dilapidated hut that could not have been more than one hundred square feet. The hut had no plumbing or electricity. And the floor was packed earth. But by the end of the day, she had a new tin roof over her head and new mud walls. And by her reaction, you would have thought we had just built her mansion in heaven!

That day was one of the most memorable days of my life because it was one of the most physically challenging days I've ever experienced. Our day started shortly after dawn, and we worked until well past dusk. We mixed the mud and hay with our feet. It was like twelve hours on a StairMaster at maximum incline. My quads were screaming. And it was backbreaking work. We carried the mud without the help of wheelbarrows and threw the mud on the walls with our bare hands. By the time we were done, my entire body smelled and looked like that clay-colored mud.

As I fell asleep that night, I had such a sense of spiritual satisfaction that I cannot put it into words. I was absolutely exhausted, but I felt like it was as close as I'd ever come to fulfilling one-quarter of the greatest commandment: "Love the Lord your God with all your...strength."[113]

I'm guessing Jonathan collapsed into bed after climbing that cliff and fighting the Philistines. Every muscle ached as he replayed the events of the day in his mind's eye. He was never more exhausted. But he was also never more energized. He experienced the holy rush of adrenaline that is a by-product of coming out of the cage and chasing the Wild Goose.

SPECTATOR SPORT

"Saul was staying on the outskirts of Gibeah under a pomegranate tree in Migron."[114]

What a study in contrasts! What Saul *didn't do* is just as significant as what Jonathan *did do*. While his son was climbing cliffs and engaging the Enemy, Saul was sitting under a pomegranate tree on the outskirts of Gibeah. I have a mental image of Saul plopping pomegranate seeds into his mouth while fanning himself with palm leaves.

Do you see what's wrong with this picture?

The Philistines controlled the pass at Micmash. And as leader of the army of Israel, Saul should have been fighting back instead of kicking back. But Saul was sitting on the sidelines instead of fighting on the front lines. And it's not the only time. Saul was also sitting on the sidelines when David fought Goliath. So let me just call it like I see it. Saul was a spiritual spectator.[115] Instead of playing to win, Saul was playing not to lose. Saul was a spectator in the game of life. He was content with letting others fight his battles for him.

I want this to come across as more of a challenge than a criticism, but I'm afraid we've turned church into a spectator sport. Too many of us are content with letting a spiritual leader seek God for us. Like the Israelites, we want Moses to climb the mountain for us.[116] After all, it is much easier to let someone else pray for us or study for us. So the church unintentionally fosters a subtle form of spiritual codependency.

I certainly believe that church plays an important role in the spiritual rhythm of our lives.[117] And we experience a unique synergy when we come together as Christ followers and worship God corporately. But do you really think God's ultimate dream for your life is to see you sit in a pew for ninety minutes every week listening to a message and singing a few songs? Is that the barometer of spiritual maturity? No way!

I wonder if we've forgotten that when we leave church we don't leave the presence of God. We take the presence of God with us wherever He leads.

It is so easy to turn church into an end instead of a means to an end. We go to church and think we've done our religious duty. We learn more and do less, all the while thinking we're fulfilling God's plan for our lives.

Spiritual spectatorship takes many forms, and some of them actually seem noble. For example, I believe that giving to missions is the greatest financial investment we can make. But like everything else, it can be done for the right reasons or for wrong reasons. Sometimes I wonder if we write a check just to ease our conscience. We give so someone else will go. But if God is calling us to go, and if all we do is give, then giving is actually a form of disobedience.

I think there is a little Saul in each of us. Part of us wants God to defeat the enemy while we sit under a pomegranate tree on the outskirts of Gibeah. We want God to do something for us without our having to do anything for God. But if we don't do anything, nothing will happen.

You've got to take the initiative. You've got to climb the cliff. You've got to pick a fight.

THE DOMINO EFFECT

On October 31, 1517, a monk named Martin Luther picked a fight. He had the audacity to challenge the status quo by attacking the selling of indulgences (get-out-of-jail-free cards for sinners). Luther posted ninety-five theses on the doors of the Castle Church in Wittenberg, Germany, and ignited the Protestant Reformation.

I'm neither a historian nor the son of a historian, but let me make an observation. Small acts of courage change the course of history. Someone does something gutsy, and it has a domino effect. I don't think Martin Luther knew he was making history as he made history. He was just doing what he believed was right regardless of circumstances or consequences.

There comes a time when enough is enough. You get tired of playing not to lose. You get tired of maintaining the status quo. You get tired of making decisions based on personal comfort. And that is when you need to stand up, step in, or step out.

At the Diet of Worms in 1521, Martin Luther was summoned by the Holy Roman emperor, Charles V, and put on trial for his beliefs. But instead of recanting, Martin Luther mustered the moral courage to take a stand. "My conscience is taken captive by God's Word, I cannot and will not recant anything. For to act against our conscience is neither safe for us, nor open to us. On this I take my stand. I can do no other. God help me. Amen."

Now let me bring it closer to home. What cliff do you need to climb? Where do you need to start standing up instead of backing down? What small act of courage could change the course of your life?

As my friend Craig Groeschel, pastor of LifeChurch.tv, says, "The difference between where you are and where God wants you to be may be the painful decision you refuse to make."

SMART COURAGE

Before going any further, I'd better make a distinction between two kinds of courage: dumb courage and smart courage. I'm certainly not advocating the kind of courage that requires lots of guts and very little intelligence.

When I was in high school, I drove a car that was affectionately known as the Batmobile. But don't let the name fool you. It was a 1984 Dodge Colt. And I'm not sure what kind of engine it had, but I'm pretty sure it was either a go-cart or a lawn-mower motor! But despite its horsepower limitations, I made that car do some amazing things.

One night, after a snowstorm, I was driving through a shopping-mall parking lot with friends. The snowplows had already plowed, so huge snowbanks were positioned at random places around the lot. That's when one of my friends posed a profound question: "I wonder if cars can drive through snowbanks?" I decided to find out. I backed up about fifty yards, got up to about forty miles per hour, and...well, my friends told me it was the most amazing explosion they had ever seen. Imagine a well-shaken snow globe, and you'll get the picture.

I discovered that, no, you cannot drive through a snowbank. And if you try it (which I don't recommend), your car will probably end up on top of the snowbank at an awkward angle. And when the tow-truck driver sees your vehicle, there will be a quizzical expression on his face: *How in the world did that car get up there?*

It took lots of courage for me to drive into that snowbank—lots of dumb courage! Dumb courage is risking something for nothing. There is no forethought. And there is no gain. It's the kind of courage that doesn't consider the consequences.

Smart courage, on the other hand, counts the costs, assesses risk/reward ratios, and practices due diligence. It's not mindless. It's mindful. And after all the consequences are considered, it does the right thing regardless of the circumstances.

I have no idea what the odds were against Jonathan and his armor-bearer. But Jonathan knew what he was up against. And he knew that he and his father were the only ones in all of Israel with swords.[118] So if he didn't challenge the status quo, who would? It was a death-defying decision but not a mindless one. The personal risk was great. He and his armor-bearer could die on the field of battle. But the reward outweighed the risk.

PLAYING OFFENSE

If you are going to chase the Wild Goose, you need to play offense with your life. Playing not to lose won't cut it. You've got to play to win!

At some point in your spiritual journey, you have to make the decision to come out of the cage. You have to stop living defensively and start living dangerously for the cause of Christ. You have to stop repeating the past and start creating the future. You have to stop letting life happen to you and start making it happen.

Ted Leonsis is a prominent Washingtonian who made his fortune as an executive with AOL. He is highly regarded as an entrepreneur and philanthropist. And he owns one of our local sports franchises, the Washington Capitals hockey team.

Ted is incredibly accomplished, but let me tell you how he got there. It was a near-death experience that put him on the offensive. In 1983 twenty-five-year-old Ted Leonsis was on an Eastern Airlines flight that lost the ability to use its wing flaps and landing gear. As flight attendants prepared the cabin for a crash-landing, Ted began thinking about what he would do if he survived. "I promised myself that if I didn't die," he reported later, "I'd play offense for the rest of my life."

Leonsis survived the landing and made good on his promise. He compiled a list of 101 life goals.[119] To date, Leonsis has checked seventy-four goals off his original list. And these are not your garden-variety goals. They are big, hairy, audacious goals.[120] Here are some of the goals Ted Leonsis has already accomplished:

- ⊗ Create the world's largest media company.
- ⊗ Own a jet.
- ⊗ Give $1 million to Georgetown University.
- ⊗ Start a family foundation.
- ⊗ Own a sports franchise.

- Produce a TV show.
- Hold elective office.
- Have a net worth of $100 million after taxes. (For the record, I'd be happy with $100 million *before* taxes!)

I love Leonsis's life-goal list. In fact, it inspired me to come up with my own list of life goals.[121] And I'd encourage you to come up with your own life-goal list. I think it's one practical way to give expression to Leonsis's motto: "Play offense with your life."

You know why most of us aren't playing offense with our lives? It's simple. We don't have any goals. I know that not everyone has a goal-setting personality. But if you've read this far, I feel like I can push you a little further: lack of goals is lack of faith. The Bible says, "Faith is being sure of what we hope for."[122] But most of us are more sure of what we're afraid of than what we hope for.

You know why most of us never accomplish what we want? Because we don't know what we want. We want to be successful. Yet we've never even taken the time to define what success would look like occupationally, relationally, or spiritually.

According to one biblical proverb, "Where there is no vision, the people perish."[123] The word *perish* refers to fruit that is past its prime. It is no longer ripening; it is rotting. A God-ordained vision is a supernatural preservative. It doesn't just keep us young; it keeps us on the offensive.

You need a vision for your marriage. You need a vision for your family. You need a vision for your career. And you need a vision for life.

Too many of us live by default instead of by design. So we go through life playing defense instead of offense. But here's what I know for sure: you won't accomplish any of the goals you do not set.

Now, I'm certainly not advocating that you go out and set a bunch of selfish goals. If you do, God won't bless them and you'd be better off spiritually if you didn't accomplish them. I'm not talking about goals that are manufactured in the human mind. I'm talking about faith goals that are inspired by God in the context of prayer. The driving motivation has to be maximizing your God-given potential. And the ultimate goal has to be to glorify God.

Make no mistake. Selfish ambition is bad.[124] But godly ambition is good. I've never met anyone who was overly ambitious for the things of God. We need to dream God-sized dreams. And it's not because we need to make a name for ourselves—selfish goals always result in shallow victories. We need to dream God-sized dreams because they're the only things that will drive us to our knees and keep us living in absolute dependence upon God the way we were designed to.

Can I share a personal conviction? I think vision is the cure for sin. One reason many of us get entangled in sin is because we don't have enough God-ordained vision to keep us busy. The more vision you have, the less you will sin. And the less vision you have, the more you will sin. It is a vision from God that keeps us playing offense spiritually.

Too often we try to stop sinning by not sinning. That is what psychologists call a double bind. It's sort of like saying, "Be spontaneous." You can't be spontaneous now that I've told you to be! The way to stop sinning is not by focusing on not sinning. The way to stopping sinning is by getting a God-sized vision that consumes all your time and energy.

THE GREAT CAUSE

I know what you may be thinking: I buy into the "play offense with your life" idea, but I'm not Jonathan.

I realize that not everyone can be a Jonathan. But all of us can at least be armor-bearers. I love the armor-bearer's response to Jonathan's challenge: "Go ahead; I am with you heart and soul."[125] Without the armor-bearer, Jonathan would have never climbed the cliff.

You can't get where God wants you to go all by yourself. For what it's worth, most of my life goals involve my wife and kids. Why? Because accomplishing something together turns a goal into a co-mission.

I want to challenge you to come up with a life-goal list. But I also want to remind you that you are part of the greatest goal ever set. I don't know that we tend to think of Jesus as a goal setter. But no one dreamed bigger dreams than Jesus. I know of no greater goal or bigger goal than the goal set by Jesus of Nazareth in the first century: "Go into all the world and proclaim the Good News to everyone, everywhere."[126]

What a God-sized goal!

We call it the Great Commission, but if it helps, think of it as the Great Vision. The moment we put our faith in Christ, we have a goal to go after. We become part of something that is far bigger and far more important than us.

You may be struggling to define success and set goals. You may not know what you want. You may feel like the compass needle is spinning as you chase the Wild Goose. I just want to remind you that you are part of the greatest dream ever dreamt.

So live with some good old-fashioned guts. Quit playing defense and start playing offense!

YOUR CHASE

- ⊛ When it comes to doing the will of God, would you say that you are more afraid of missing opportunities than of making mistakes? Why or why not?

- ⊛ Think of a time in the past when you did something daring for God. What was the outcome? How do you feel about the experience as you look back?

- ⊛ What is something daring you'd like to do for God now? What fears stand in the way of your doing it? What do you think God would like to say to you about those fears?

- ⊛ Do you have a life-goal list? If you do, what is on it? If not, what would be the first ten goals you'd like to put on such a list?

- ⊛ As you're pursuing a God-sized vision, where does your Wild Goose chase go from here?

Madonna of the Future

> My deepest belief is that living as if you are
> dying sets us free.
>
> —Anne Lamott

Henry James once wrote a story titled "The Madonna of the Future" about an artist who devotes her entire life to a single painting. But when the artist dies, it is discovered that her canvas is still blank. She never finished because she never started.

Lord Acton, a nineteenth-century historian, borrowed James's phrase to describe his own lifework. This notable thinker (famous in DC circles for his aphorism "Power tends to corrupt, and absolute power corrupts absolutely") authored numerous lectures, essays, and reviews. But he never published a book. In fact, he referred to his lifework, *A History of Liberty,* as his "Madonna of the Future." And it is described by many as "the greatest book that was never written." In the words of Daniel Boorstin, Lord Acton was "always discouraged by the imperfection of the material, he always delayed his unifying work by the promise of new facts and new ideas still to come."[127] Boorstin said Lord Acton knew too much to write. And thus his lifework, the culmination of everything he'd learned and experienced, became a "Madonna of the Future."

So here's my question: what is your unpainted canvas or unwritten book? What God-given dream is collecting dust? What God-ordained passion remains caged?

I have no idea what your "Madonna of the Future" is. But here's what I do know: you'll never finish what you do not start. And that is where so many of us get stuck. We fail to take the first step, so the Wild Goose chase never even begins. Instead of seeking out adventure, we settle for routine. Instead of playing offense with our lives, we play defense. And instead of living by faith, we let our fears dictate our decisions.

THE LAST DAY OF YOUR LIFE

I've always loved Frederick Buechner's perspective on life. He said, "Today is the first day of your life because it has never been before, and today is the last day of your life because it will never be again." What a great perspective on today. And what a great approach to life!

What if we treated each day as the first day and last day of our lives? How would it change the way we treat the people around us? How would it change the way we spend our time? How would it change the way we prioritize our lives?

In stark contrast to Lord Acton, Évariste Galois stands as a testament to what can be accomplished in a single day. On May 29, 1832,

Galois sat down and wrote a sixty-page mathematical masterpiece from start to finish in one sitting. In one night he accomplished more than most people do in a lifetime. "What he wrote in those desperate long hours before dawn," according to Eric Bell, "will keep generations of mathematicians busy for hundreds of years."[128]

So how did Galois do it? Well, here's the rest of the story. Pescheux d'Herbinville[129] had challenged Galois to a duel, and Galois knew it might be his last chance to leave a legacy. He treated May 29, 1832, as if it were the last day of his life. In the margins of the paper he scribbled several times, "I have not time, I have not time." He wrote frantically, finishing three hours before dawn.

Galois died from gunshot wounds the next day.

Death has a unique way of bringing a sense of desperation and definition to our lives, doesn't it? It focuses our faculties. It defines our priorities. And in some strange way, the imminence of death intensifies life. So why do so many of us wait until we're close to dying to really start living?

What are we waiting for?

I've already stated that I don't think your date of death is necessarily the date carved on your tombstone. Most people die long before that. And in the same sense, most people don't start living until long after the date stamped on their birth certificate—or long after they become supposedly responsible adults, for that matter. Until we come out of whatever cage holds us back, we will live unfruitful and unfulfilled lives. But start chasing the Wild Goose and you will come alive in ways you've never previously experienced. Real life and real adventure begin the moment you are born of the Spirit and begin chasing the Wild Goose.[130]

CHASING RABBITS, CHASING GOOSES

I recently read an interview with Dallas Willard in which he tells a story about a dog race that happened in Florida a few years ago. Dogs are trained to chase an electronic rabbit around a track, but one night the rabbit broke down and the dogs caught it. The funny thing is that the dogs didn't know what to do. They just stood around barking and leaping and yelping. They were utterly confused. Dallas Willard said:

> I think that's a picture of what happens to all sorts of people
> who catch the rabbit in their life. Whether it's wealth or fame
> or beauty or a bigger house, or whatever, the prize isn't what
> they thought it would be. And when they finally get it, they
> don't know what to do with their lives. This is a huge factor in
> finishing badly: people need a rabbit that won't break down.
> But that's not something the superficial values of this world
> can really give them.[131]

Ultimately, the only "rabbit" worth chasing is a goose—the Wild Goose.

Did you know that Israeli scientists have discovered a piece of genetic code (DRD4) that may explain our primal longing for adventure? And while research is ongoing, it seems that the need for adventure is part of God's genetic design. We are adventure-seeking creatures. It's the way we're wired. We need some danger, some challenge, some risk. And the only one who can completely satisfy that human longing for adventure is the One who created us with that desire in the first place: God Himself.

Every other chase besides the Wild Goose chase will leave you feeling empty. Every other chase will leave you with a gnawing feeling that something is still missing. Why? Because everything else can be caught or accomplished. But not the Wild Goose. The Wild Goose is eternally elusive. And that is why He is worthy of chasing. In the words of A. W. Tozer, "Eternity won't be long enough to learn all that God is or praise Him for all that He has done."

THE SIX CAGES REVISITED

So what's keeping you in the cage?

As you've read *Wild Goose Chase*, I hope you've not just identified the cages that keep you from the spiritual adventure God destined for you. I hope you have also identified some action steps you can take.

The Wild Goose chase begins when you come out of the *cage of responsibility* and start pursuing God-ordained passions like Nehemiah did. What makes you sad, mad, or glad? And what are you going to do about it? Too many of us allow our human responsibilities to get in the way of our primary calling: pursuing the passions God has put in our hearts. Maybe it's time to quit praying and start acting. And I promise this: if you step out in faith, confirming signs will follow.

Or maybe you've gotten stuck in the *cage of routine*. Somewhere along the way, your relationship with God became more of a chore than an adventure. Listen, if you don't disrupt the routine, you will eventually stop living and start existing. So what changes do you need to make in your life? Something as simple as a change of pace or a change of place can give you a new perspective on life. Here's my advice. Take off your sandals and throw down your staff. Take some radical steps to simplify your life. Create some margin for spiritual spontaneity. And learn to listen to God.

Undoubtedly, some of us are in the *cage of assumptions*. We place far too many eight-foot ceilings between us and God. Where have you made God in your image? And where does God need to remake you in His image? Where do you need to keep hoping against all hope? And what personal assumptions do you need to challenge? Let me say it again: you'll never be good enough or smart enough or experienced enough. But your qualifications aren't the issue. When you chase the Wild Goose, the best you can do is no longer the best you can do; the best you can do is the best God can do. And God is able to do immeasurably more than all you can ask or imagine.

One of the cages many of us find ourselves in and out of frequently is the *cage of guilt*. Satan wants to remind you of past mistakes over and over again. Why? So you don't have any emotional or spiritual energy left to dream kingdom dreams. But Jesus came to recondition our guilt with His grace. And when you receive His grace, it not only reconditions your heart but also turns you into a revolutionary for His cause. So what reactions need to be reconditioned? Is there sin in your life that needs to be confessed? And who do you need to forgive?

Somewhere in our spiritual journey, all of us land in the *cage of failure*. And how we handle it will make us or break us. When our plans fail, there is a temptation to not only give up on our dreams but also to give up on God and ourselves. But sometimes it takes a shipwreck to get you where God wants you to go. And what seems like a complete disaster will actually set a new course for your life. Tired of divine delays? Feel like your life is a divine detour? Let me remind you of three things: (1) the longer you have to wait, the more you will appreciate; (2) sometimes the most spiritual thing you can do is hang in there; and (3) a sense of humor can get you through just about anything. And one more thing, no matter how crazy the Wild Goose chase gets, don't forget to enjoy the journey!

And finally, if you're going to experience the adventure God desires and destines for you, you have to come out of the *cage of fear*. Don't let worries about the unknown dictate your decisions. Why? Because God is on your side! Make Jonathan's statement of faith your modus operandi: "Perhaps the LORD will act in our behalf." Don't play defense with your life. Play offense with your kids, your wife, your life. Don't look for the path of least resistance. The hard way is the best way! And quit living as if the will of God is an insurance plan. Dare to dream great things for God.

CALL OF THE WILD

A few months ago I was reading the writings of John Muir, the founder of the Sierra Club. Muir was an adventurer extraordinaire. He climbed mountains, crossed rivers, and explored glaciers long before GPS, 30,000-BTU camping stoves, or CamelBak hydration units.

One of my favorite Muir moments happened in December 1874. John Muir was staying with a friend at his cabin in the Sierra Nevada when a severe winter storm set in. The wind was so strong that it bent the trees over. And while most people would retreat to shelter in a situation like that, Muir came out of the cabin and walked into the storm. He found a mountain ridge, climbed to the top of a giant Douglas fir tree, and held on for dear life. For several hours, Muir feasted his senses on the sights and sounds and scents.

In his journal Muir wrote, "When the storm began to sound I lost no time in pushing out into the woods to enjoy it. For on such occasions, Nature always has something rare to show us, and the danger to life and limb is hardly greater than one would experience crouching deprecatingly beneath a roof."

I love Eugene Peterson's take on Muir's story. He said the story of John Muir climbing to the top of that storm-whipped Douglas fir is "an icon of Christian spirituality." He called it "a standing rebuke against becoming a mere spectator to life, preferring creature comfort to Creator confrontation."

You've been comfortable long enough, haven't you? Isn't it time to come out of the cage?

And remember, ultimately it's not about you. It's about the One who wants to write His-story through your life. A world in desperate need can't do without what you will bring when you become part of something that is bigger than you and more important than you: the cause of Christ in this generation. The stakes could not be higher. And like the first-century disciples, we have the opportunity to turn the world upside down.

Two thousand years ago, Jesus issued a standing invitation: follow Me. But it came with a warning: "Foxes have holes and birds of the air have nests, but the Son of Man has no place to lay his head."[132] When you embark on your Wild Goose chase, you never know where you're going to end up. Jesus never promised safety or certainty or predictability. And He certainly didn't die on the cross to tame us. He died to make us dangerous. He died to invite us into a life of spiritual adventure. And if you will have the courage to come out of the cage and chase the Wild Goose, life will turn into another day, another adventure!

Quit living as if the purpose of life is
to arrive safely at death.

Set God-sized goals.

Pursue God-ordained passions.

Go after a dream that is destined to fail
without divine intervention.

Don't let fear dictate your decisions.

Don't take the easy way out.

Don't maintain the status quo.

Stop pointing out problems and become
part of the solution.

Stop repeating the past and start
creating the future.

Stop playing not to lose and start
playing to win.

Expand your horizons.

Create some margins.

Take off your sandals.

Find every excuse you can to celebrate
everything you can.

Live today like it is the first day and
the last day of your life.

Don't let what's wrong with you keep you
from worshiping what's right with God.

Burn sinful bridges.

Challenge old assumptions.

Blaze new trails.

Don't stop making mistakes.
Celebrate your failures.

Don't try to be who you're not. Be yourself.

Don't make a living. Make a life.

Quit making excuses.

Quit playing defense.

And quit putting eight-foot ceilings
on what God can do.

Chase the Goose!

Acknowledgments

I've learned a lot of lessons since my first book, *In a Pit with a Lion on a Snowy Day*, was published. I've learned that when you write a book, people think you know more than you actually do. Trust me, I don't. For me, writing has a humbling effect. It forces me to come to terms with how much I don't know.

Writing has also helped me figure out who I am and who I'm not. And it is who I'm not that helps me appreciate the people who surround me. I owe so many thank-yous to so many people that it's hard to know where to begin.

First and foremost, I want to thank my wife and kids for putting up with the early mornings and late nights that resulted in *Wild Goose Chase*. Writing is a labor of love for me. I love it, but it definitely involves lots of labor. And my family was incredibly generous and gracious as my writing deadline approached.

I want to thank National Community Church in Washington DC for allowing me to serve as their pastor. I wouldn't want to be anyplace else doing anything else. I'm constantly inspired by our staff and leaders who are so gifted and so committed to the cause of Christ. You make my job so easy! And a special thank-you to our prayer team that prayed for me as I wrote this book. And for what it's worth, they also prayed for you!

I want to thank the entire team at WaterBrook Multnomah. Thanks for believing in me. Thanks for encouraging me. And thanks for the partnership in getting what God has put into my heart into the hands of readers. Over the past year I've received hundreds of e-mails from readers who have been impacted by *In a Pit with a Lion on a Snowy Day*. Each of you should have been CCed on all of those emails!

One of the lessons I've learned in life and ministry is that you are only as good as the people you surround yourself with. So thanks to Stephen Cobb and Ken Petersen for your leadership. Thanks to Tiffany Lauer, Allison O'Hara, and the entire marketing team for your creativity. Thanks to Joel Ruse, Leah Apineru, Lori Addicott, Alice Crider, Jessica Lacy, Elizabeth Johnson, Carie Freimuth, Joel Kneedler, Julia Wallace, and Jon Woodhams for your diligence and assistance. And a special thanks to David Kopp and Eric Stanford for your patience and brilliance in helping to shape *Wild Goose Chase*.

Notes

1. John 3:8.
2. Genesis 2:19.
3. Matthew 19:20.
4. Matthew 19:21.
5. Mark Batterson, *In a Pit with a Lion on a Snowy Day: How to Survive and Thrive When Opportunity Roars* (Colorado Springs, CO: Multnomah, 2006). The story of Benaiah is found in 2 Samuel 23:20–23.
6. Hebrews 12:2.
7. Acts 17:6, KJV.
8. Roger Highfield, *The Physics of Christmas: From the Aerodynamics of Reindeer to the Thermodynamics of Turkey* (Boston: Little, Brown, 1998), 168–69.
9. From Wilson Snowflake Bentley, http://snowflakebentley .com/ (accessed March 25 2008).
10. Stephen R. Graves and Thomas G. Addington, *The Fourth Frontier: Exploring the New World of Work* (Nashville: Word, 2000), 5.
11. Luke 9:59–60.
12. Mark 3:21.
13. Nehemiah 1:1–4, NLT.
14. Frederick Buechner, *The Hungering Dark* (San Francisco: HarperSanFrancisco, 1985), 31–32.
15. Genesis 1:4, 10, 12, 18, 21, 25, 31.

16. Nehemiah 2:4.

17. Nehemiah 2:4–5.

18. Psalm 37:4.

19. Peter Marshall, *Mr. Jones, Meet the Master!* (Old Tappan, NJ: Revell, 1988), 143–44.

20. Matthew 25:23.

21. Joshua 3:9–13.

22. Mark 16:20, KJV.

23. Nehemiah 2:7–9.

24. Nehemiah 2:1–2.

25. The passion was conceived in the month of Kislev (November–December). Nehemiah didn't verbalize the passion to the king until the month of Nisan (March–April).

26. Quoted in Jack Canfield and Mark Victor Hansen, *The Aladdin Factor* (New York: Berkley Books, 1995), 255.

27. Psalm 29:1, MSG.

28. John 14:16.

29. Exodus 3:1–5.

30. Abraham Cohen, *Everyman's Talmud* (New York: Schocken Books, 1995), 8–9.

31. Mark 4:35–39.

32. Mark 9:2.

33. Don't know where to start? I have a friend named Brian Mosley who runs an amazing organization called the Right-Now Campaign. They are a clearinghouse for mission organizations. Check them out at www.rightnow.org.

34. Psalm 46:10.

35. Luke 10:25–37.

36. John Darley and C. Daniel Batson, "From Jerusalem to Jericho: A Study of Situational and Dispositional Variables in Helping Behavior," *Journal of Personality and Social Psychology* 27 (1973): 100–108.

37. Mark 10:47–48.

38. Mark 10:49.

39. Isaiah 29:13, NLT.

40. Matthew 6:7–8, NLT.

41. Exodus 4:2–5.

42. Exodus 3:11.

43. Exodus 3:12.

44. Matthew 14:22–33.

45. Doron Nof, Ian McKeague, and Nathan Paldor, "Is There a Paleolimnological Explanation for 'Walking on Water' in the Sea of Galilee?" *Journal of Paleolimnology* 35 (2006): 417–39. Available online at http://doronnof.net/files/kinneret.pdf (accessed March 25 2008).

46. Genesis 1:27.

47. A. W. Tozer, *The Knowledge of the Holy* (HarperCollins: New York, 1978), 43.

48. Genesis 15:5.

49. William Beebe, *The Book of Naturalists: An Anthology of Best Natural History* (Princeton, NJ: Princeton University Press, 1988), 234.

50. 1 Corinthians 8:2.

51. Matthew 7:7.

52. Matthew 19:26.

53. Rolf Smith, *The Seven Levels of Change: The Guide to Innovation in the World's Largest Corporations* (Arlington, TX: Summit, 1997), 49.

54. Matthew 18:3.

55. Pat Williams with Jim Denney, *The Paradox of Power: A Transforming View of Leadership* (New York: Warner, 2002), 19–20.

56. Romans 4:18–21.

57. John 2:4.

58. Philippians 4:13.

59. Ephesians 3:20.

60. Malachi 3:10.

61. Luke 6:38.

62. Genesis 14:17–24.

63. Genesis 21:1–7.

64. Genesis 18:12.

65. Genesis 18:14.

66. Hebrews 11:8.

67. Peter Marshall and David Manuel, *The Light and the Glory* (Old Tappan, NJ: Fleming H. Revell, 1977), 17.

68. Hebrews 8:12.

69. Luke 22:54–62.

70. 1 Peter 5:8.

71. Revelation 12:10.

72. 1 Timothy 1:15 KJV.

73. Matthew 5:39, 41, 44; Luke 6:27–28.

74. 1 Peter 3:9.

75. Luke 22:31–32.

76. John 8:4–5.

77. John 8:7.

78. John 8:11.

79. Romans 5:8.

80. Matthew 18:21–22, NLT.

81. Luke 22:61.

82. John 18:10.

83. I want to thank my friend and mentor Dick Foth for his insight into this passage. The ideas I share in this section are his.

84. 2 Corinthians 5:21.

85. Genesis 3:8.

86. 1 John 1:9.

87. James 5:16.

88. Mark 2:17.

89. John 21:3.

90. John 21:15–17.

91. John 21:4.

92. Acts 28:1–4, NLT.

93. Acts 28:5–10, NLT.

94. Luke 23:40–41.

95. Luke 23:42–43.

96. John 16:33.

97. Proverbs 16:9.

98. Acts 27:3, 7, 13, 15, 18.

99. John 3:8.

100. Revelation 3:7–8.

101. Isaiah 22:20–24.

102. John 10:9, ESV.

103. Oswald Chambers, *My Utmost for His Highest* (Westwood, NJ: Barbour and Co., 1963), 152.

104. Philippians 1:6.

105. 1 Corinthians 3:7.

106. William J. Gehring and Adrian R. Willoughby, "The Medial Frontal Cortex and the Rapid Processing of Monetary Gains and Losses," *Science* 295, no. 5563 (March 22, 2002): 2279–82. Available online at http://www.sciencemag.org/cgi/content/abstract/295/5563/2279.

107. 1 Samuel 14:1–6.

108. 1 Samuel 14:10.

109. 1 Samuel 14:6.

110. 1 Samuel 14:23.

111. Matthew 11:12, KJV.

112. Matthew 11:12.

113. Mark 12:30.

114. 1 Samuel 14:2.

115. Some of these thoughts were originally inspired by Erwin McManus and his book *Seizing Your Divine Moments*.

116. Exodus 20:18–19.

117. Hebrews 10:25.

118. 1 Samuel 13:22.

119. See Ted Leonsis's list of life goals at http://www.superviva.com/idea-lists/4-Ted-Leonsis-039-Famous-List.html (accessed March 25 2008).

120. "Big, hairy, audacious goals" is a term used in James C. Collins and Jerry I. Porras, *Built to Last: Successful Habits of Visionary Companies* (New York: HarperBusiness, 1994).

121. You can find my life-goal list at www.markbatterson.com.

122. Hebrews 11:1.

123. Proverbs 29:18, KJV.

124. Philippians 2:3.

125. 1 Samuel 14:7.

126. Mark 16:15, NLT.

127. Daniel J. Boorstin, *The Seekers: The Story of Man's Continuing Quest to Understand His World* (New York: Random House, 1998), 235.

128. Eric T. Bell, *Men of Mathematics* (New York: Simon & Schuster, 1937), 375.

129. While the identity of the person who challenged Galois is surrounded by some historical uncertainty, Alexandre Dumas names Pescheux d'Herbinville.

130. John 3:8.

131. Dallas Willard quoted by Robert Buford, "Is There Something More? A Conversation to Remember," Career Planning & Adult Development Network *Network Newsletter*, January/February 2005 (http://www.careernetwork.org/carccr_nsltrbufordjf05.html, accessed April 25, 2008.)

132. Matthew 8:20.

Don't miss out on the FREE resources available on these sites ideal for sermon series or small group studies:

- Short films
- Bookmarks
- Graphics
- Posters

And MORE...

www.chasethegoose.com

www.chasethelion.com

About *In a Pit With a Lion on a Snowy Day*

What if the life you really want, and the future God wants for you, is hiding right now in your biggest problem, your worst failure... your greatest fear? *In a Pit with a Lion on a Snowy Day,* inspired by one of the most obscure yet courageous acts recorded in Scripture (2 Samuel 23:20-21) will help you to unleash the lion chaser within!

Visit Mark's blog: www.markbatterson.com